JAN KRENTZ

DIAMOND QUILTS & BEYOND

FROM THE BASICS TO DAZZLING DESIGNS

C&T PUBLISHING INC.

Text © 2005 Jan Krentz
Artwork © 2005 C&T Publishing
Publisher: Amy Marson
Editorial Director: Gailen Runge
Acquisitions Editor: Jan Grigsby
Editor: Liz Aneloski
Technical Editors: Carolyn Aune, Cynthia Keyes Hilton
Copyeditor/Proofreader: Wordfirm Inc.
Cover Designer: Kristy Zacharias
Book Designer: Staci Harpole, Cubic Design
Illustrator: Kirstie McCormick
Production Assistant: Matt Allen
Quilt Photography: Carina Woolrich
How-to Photography: Luke Mulks, unless otherwise noted
Stock Photography on pages 15, 19, 25, 26, 30, 32, and 99 courtesy of Corel Professional Images;
pages 19, 22, 23, 24, 25, 26, 58, and 61 courtesy of Comstock Images; pages 12, 13, 16, 17, 18,
19, 31, 32 and 113 courtesy of PhotoSpin; pages 15, 18, 24, and 30 courtesy of Corbis.
Published by C&T Publishing, Inc., P.O. Box 1456, Lafayette, CA 94549

Front cover: *Monet Water Lily*, Jan Krentz
Back cover: *Advent Calendar*, Suzanne Kistler and *Botanical Magnolia Stellata*, Kathy Butler

Krentz, Jan P.
  Diamond quilts & beyond : from the basics to dazzling designs / Jan
Krentz.
      p. cm.
  Includes index.
  ISBN 1-57120-240-4 (paper trade)
  1. Patchwork--Patterns. 2. Quilting. 3. Patchwork quilts--Design. 4.
Landscape in art. I. Title: Diamond quilts and beyond. II. Title.

  TT835.K7596 2005
  746.46'041--dc22

2004023981

Printed in China
10 9 8 7 6 5 4 3 2 1

Acknowledgments

Sincerest thanks to the quiltmakers—
their artistry makes this book a treasure!

Betty Alofs
Mona Baran
Priscilla Bianchi
Edie Brown
Kathy Butler
Christina Cormier
Mary Beth Craig
Barbara Engler
Jude Ferris
Charlotte Freeman
Laura Lee Fritz
Jacqué Holmes
Pam Kay
Suzanne Kistler
Jan Kolarov
Lynne Lichtenstern
Gloria Loughman
Carol Coor-Pender McCrea
D'Andrea Mitchell
Alison Morton
Patricia Nichols
Bettie Ratner
Carolyn Reynolds
Patricia Richie
T.G. Custom Quilting
Toni Silvera
Lisa Taylor
Kathryn and Stu Veltkamp
Patricia Votruba
Sandra Wagner
Cassandra Williams
Ruth Wolf

My appreciation to Pfaff Sewing Machine
Company for their fine machines. I have
sewn all of my quilts on Pfaff sewing
machines since 1980.

With recognition and appreciation to the
professional editors and artists at C&T
Publishing—you are amazing!

Thanks to Patty and Louis Herzog for
the lovely, secluded oasis in the woods—
it was the perfect place to write.

With love to my family—
Don, Ryan, Dan, and Lindsay Krentz

Contents

Preface

As a quiltmaker, instructor, and designer, I enjoy creating quilts that incorporate a variety of techniques. When I work on a single design, multiple variations develop, with each successive quilt more exciting than the previous one!

While I developed designs for my two previous books, Lone Stars & Beyond and Hunter Stars & Beyond, the current pieced and embellished landscape quilts emerged. The 45° diamond is a simple geometric shape with a variety of design applications. Based on historic charm quilts, Diamond Quilts & Beyond blends traditional construction techniques, contemporary fabrics, and artful embellishments.

Welcome to this quilt adventure, which includes everything from traditional geometric designs to those with an impressionistic flair. Incorporate your favorite techniques to create a quilted masterpiece to treasure for years to come.

Happy Stitching!

Jan P. Krentz

Introduction

I have been fascinated by eight-pointed star quilts for many years. The geometric shapes within a true eight-pointed star—45° diamonds, squares, and right triangles—are key ingredients in most traditional quilt blocks. During the research for my first book, *Lone Star Quilts & Beyond*, I realized the design potential of the 45° diamond (also known as a parallelogram).

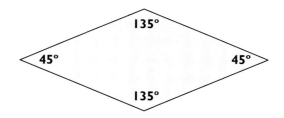

45° DIAMOND (PARALLELOGRAM)

LONE STAR QUILT DESIGN

Single-unit quilt designs have historically been known as charm quilts. Quilters challenged themselves to collect hundreds of calico fabrics, striving to create an entire quilt without repeating any single fabric. Geometric shapes such as squares, rectangles, hexagons, equilateral (60°) triangles, right triangles (also known today as half-square or quarter-square triangles), and 60° and 45° diamonds were ideal for charm quilts.

PIECED CLAMSHELLS (CIRCA 1800), COLLECTION OF PAT NICHOLS

PIECED SQUARES, PAM KAY

PIECED RECTANGLES IN AN OFFSET OR BRICK LAYOUT, COLLECTION OF PAM KAY

ANTIQUE STRING-PIECED DIAMONDS, COLLECTION OF BARBARA ENGLER

PIECED RECTANGLES IN A HERRINGBONE LAYOUT, PAM KAY

PIECED EQUILATERAL 60° TRIANGLES, ALISON MORTON

PIECED 60° DIAMONDS, COLLECTION OF PAT NICHOLS

PIECED HEXAGONS IN A SYMMETRICAL LAYOUT, RUTH WOLF

PIECED 45° DIAMONDS, COLLECTION OF PAT NICHOLS

A simple pieced pattern is created when the diamonds are oriented in horizontal or vertical symmetrical rows. This pattern of repeating diamonds is relatively simple to construct, enabling the quilter to create beautiful, artistic pieced backgrounds. The designs may be further embellished with appliqué, surface thread work, beading, and quilting.

HORIZONTAL DIAMOND ROWS
DETAIL OF *MONET WATER LILY* (FULL QUILT ON PAGE 98)

VERTICAL DIAMOND ROWS
DETAIL OF *MORNING STAR'S GARDEN* BY CHRISTINA CORMIER
(FULL QUILT ON PAGE 111)

DETAIL OF *TAMSEN LAKE* BY JAN KOLAROV (FULL QUILT ON PAGE 69)

DETAIL OF *REFLECTIONS FROM SWAN LAKE* BY MARY BETH CRAIG
(FULL QUILT ON PAGE 93)

DETAIL OF *POND LIFE* BY PATRICIA RICHIE
(FULL QUILT ON PAGES 70–71)

INSPIRATION
AND
DESIGN

Inspiration & Design

Design inspiration surrounds us! We view landscapes, gardens, mountain vistas, seashores, trees, cityscapes, cultivated fields, produce departments, rows of merchandise for sale, paintings in a gallery, children at play, bouquets of flowers, sunsets, athletic events, and much more. Calendars, magazines, travel brochures, greeting cards, and books carry images that capture our imagination and strike the chord of our creative souls.

PAINTINGS

Invest several hours in studying various styles of paintings. Visit your public library's art section, browse contemporary art magazines, or search the Internet. Doing so will help you absorb the concepts needed to create your own exciting compositions with unpredictable splashes of color and texture. The most vibrant images and subject matter are those that have personal meaning to you.

You can start by studying the paintings of the following artists:

Impressionists (circa 1830–1926):
Mary Cassatt
Edgar Degas
Édouard Manet
Claude Monet
Berthe Morisot
Camille Jacob Pissarro
Pierre-Auguste Renoir
Alfred Sisley

Postimpressionists (circa 1839–1953):
Paul Cézanne
William Merritt Chase
Raoul Dufy
Paul Gauguin
J. B. Armand Guillaumin
Henri Rousseau
Georges Seurat
Henri de Toulouse-Lautrec
Vincent van Gogh

Cubists (circa 1881–1973):
Georges Braque
Pablo Picasso

Contemporary Artists (circa 1927–present):
LeRoy Neiman
Georgia O'Keefe

THE RIVERBANK, LA GRENOUILLERE BY VINCENT VAN GOGH

THE STARRY NIGHT BY VINCENT VAN GOGH

LANDSCAPE OF ILE DE FRANCE BY PAUL CEZANNE

OLD ST. LAZARRE STATION BY CLAUDE MONET

BRIDGE AT ARGENTEUIL BY CLAUDE MONET

FISHERMAN'S COTTAGE ON THE CLIFFS AT VARENGEVILLE BY CLAUDE MONET

PHOTOGRAPHS

Our albums are filled with photographs of friends, relatives, homes, and pets that we hold dear to our lives. Perhaps you have photos of your childhood home, a favorite vacation spot, or a honeymoon vista. You may also have sketches, doodles, drawings, or original artwork that may serve as the foundation for a wonderful quilt design.

Find inspiration for your work by looking at your photographs of special events, scenery, or everyday surroundings. Successful compositions incorporate a variety of subject matter—landscapes, gardens, architecture, people, bodies of water, or still lifes of everyday items.

Determine the depth of the composition—close-up, midrange, or panoramic. Is the subject complete, or does it require more detail in the foreground or background?

LUPINE FLOWERS WITH BACKGROUND DETAIL

LUPINE FLOWERS WITH FORE-, MIDDLE-, AND BACKGROUND DETAIL

LUPINE FLOWERS IN A FIELD

When seeking images, the best approach is to work with your own photography whenever possible. Benefits include:

- ◆ Artistic freedom to zoom in on the subject
- ◆ The ability to supplement the subject with additional design elements
- ◆ The option to produce original designs of subjects that interest you
- ◆ The opportunity to become more knowledgeable about your quilt's subject matter

If your design is based on a commercial photograph, you must secure permission from the photographer or copyright holder.

COPYRIGHT ISSUES

Any printed, painted, or published image, document, article, photograph, or drawing usually carries a copyright held by the maker/artist, a company, a museum, a corporate entity, or a publisher. You must contact the appropriate copyright holder and secure written permission before rendering any image into a quilt.

ENGLISH GARDEN AND COTTAGE

GARDEN LANDSCAPES

Landscape designers are skilled professionals. Beautiful gardens flourish in most countries, and many of us are fortunate to live near a botanical garden, city park, natural forest, or a neighbor's garden. Take a break from your daily life and, with camera in hand, visit the local parks or gardens. Observe natural and cultivated landscapes from a distance. Study the varying appearance of plants, trees, hills, and mountains close to you. Note how they change as they recede from view.

CASUAL FLOWER FIELDS AND WINDMILLS

A SIMPLE BRIDGE IN A LOVELY GARDEN

PERSPECTIVE

Perspective is an aspect of the natural world that is observed every day, yet we are rarely *aware* of the light and shadow that define form, structure, shape, supple curves, or rigid straight edges. We instinctively view and understand the dimensional properties of trees, flowers, plains, rock formations, cliffs, clouds, bodies of water, and all other natural images in our surroundings without consciously *seeing* them.

REMOTE CASTLE REFLECTED IN SURROUNDING WATER

MOUNTAIN VISTA GLIMPSED THROUGH OVERHANGING TREE BRANCHES

When creating a design, the perspectives of buildings, landscapes, and other elements must relate to one another or the design will have a primitive, surrealistic, or cartoon-like appearance. Artists are trained to observe the characteristics of each subject and render the subject to appear in proportion and perspective. Artistic license allows us to simplify a scene, add color and intensity where little may exist, or combine elements from a variety of sources to create an entire image.

LANDSCAPES— NATURAL VISTAS

Depending on where you live, landscapes may be small-town scenes, agricultural fields, geologic vistas, or architectural cityscapes. Observe your surroundings with an artist's eye to discover ideal quilt designs in your daily environment.

A LONG-RANGE VIEW OF THE PLAINS, WILDLIFE, FOLIAGE, AND CLOUDS

RED BERRIES ON A LEAFLESS BRANCH

CLOSE-UP DETAIL OF A BUTTERFLY ON PINK BLOSSOMS

PINE NEEDLES ON A FOGGY MORNING

Regardless of the subject matter, rendering images in cloth is a worthwhile and daunting task. Where to begin?

BUILD AN IMAGE FILE

Label file folders with the design features that interest you. Examples of file subjects are listed below. If you have collected images of a large number of topics, you could divide them into subcategories, creating files for each subcategory. This list is not complete; please add your own categories!

- ◆ Flowers
- ◆ Animals sorted by continent
- ◆ People
- ◆ Mountains
- ◆ Sky
- ◆ Water
- ◆ Aquatic life
- ◆ Birds
- ◆ Insects
- ◆ Color
- ◆ Texture
- ◆ Geometric patterns/designs

TRAVEL

The opportunity to travel and explore communities, states, and countries has never been greater. Become a photojournalist, recording the new experiences outside your daily life and surroundings. Store the images in files sorted by subject matter.

FILE FOLDERS ORGANIZED BY CATEGORY

COLLECT ITEMS THAT INSPIRE YOUR CREATIVITY.

CHOOSE A THEME

Select a favorite location—for instance, your childhood home in the spring season. Visualize the location. Perhaps you are working from a photograph to help provide details. Will the home be in the center of the quilt, with blooming flowers in front or budding leafy trees surrounding it? Draw a few sketches— just rough ideas with the overall shape of the quilt (square? rectangular? wide? tall?) and the location of the house within the quilt. Determine whether the house will fill the quilt; whether it will be centered, right, left, top, or bottom; and so on. Will there be lots of surrounding details—landscaping, background hills, or sky? Make several rough sketches until you are comfortable with the design layout. Begin refining the design, adding detail, working out fabric selections, and determining what methods you would like to use for constructing the design.

If you are working with a particular subject, such as a flower, the design process is similar.

Determine the following quilt attributes:

♦ Finished size/shape of the quilt composition

Will it be rectangular, square, vertical, horizontal, or irregularly shaped?

♦ Position of the key elements

Will they be centered, right, left, higher, or lower in the quilt?

♦ Size of the key subject(s)

Will it be large, filling the composition with a close-up magnification, as in Georgia O'Keeffe's flower paintings?

Will it be medium, filling a portion of the quilt with, say, a bouquet or view of several flowers and leaving room for surrounding foliage and background?

Will it be small, with scattered, profuse clusters of the same element, such as flowers in a field or garden? The background itself will become the primary subject, and the flowers will be the secondary subjects.

CREATING A DESIGN BACKGROUND

Once you have chosen a theme, you will need to decide if your quilt will be horizontal or vertical in orientation and small, medium, or large in size. Does the finished quilt need to fit a particular location?

Sketch a loose format for the diamond-grid background, determining where the larger areas of color will be located. If you are creating a garden landscape, you might include dark areas for shrubbery, blue for sky, dappled-green fabrics for trees, or possibly a winding path area. Simplicity is the key for these areas of color.

Next, create a diamond-grid background. After you piece the background, additional design elements in appliqué will flesh out the theme, supporting and filling in the composition. In a garden example, flowers, leaves, a park bench, birds, or a gazebo could be added to the pieced background, further enhancing the quilt.

PIECED DIAMOND BACKGROUNDS

Diamonds or parallelograms lend themselves to purely geometric designs. The angled seams create visually dynamic lines within a quilted composition, allowing you to sew simple pieced backgrounds with visual appeal. Sew collections of patterned fabrics, merging and blending fabric designs together from row to row.

A DIAMOND GEOMETRIC DESIGN IN *DIAMONDS GALORE* BY CAROL COOR-PENDER MCCREA

WOVEN DIAMOND BACKGROUNDS

A simple, effective method for creating diamond backgrounds is to weave ribbons at an angle. The finished edges of the ribbons create a stable surface without raveling. The shimmering surfaces catch the light, creating an elegant background for appliqué or machine-embroidery motifs.

Woven ribbon designs intended for use as clothing or embellishment on pillows, purses, or quilts have greater stability when the layers are secured with stitching. Woven compositions may be framed and protected by glass. Wallhanging designs may be covered with a sheer layer of tulle or organza.

A DIAMOND GEOMETRIC DESIGN EXPRESSES A HOLIDAY THEME IN *ADVENT CALENDAR* BY SUZANNE KISTLER (FULL QUILT ON PAGE 68).

A WOVEN RIBBON FRAME ENHANCES *RIBBONS OF SPRING* BY PATRICIA VOTRUBA (FULL QUILT ON PAGE 87).

A SIMPLE PANEL WOVEN OF SHEER RIBBONS CREATES AN EXCITING DESIGN. MAINTAINING THE ANGLES IN BOTH DIRECTIONS CREATES A CONSISTENT PATTERN.

A DIAMOND DESIGN IN *AURORA SENTINEL* BY JACQUÉ HOLMES HAS A PAINTED APPEARANCE (FULL QUILT ON PAGE 81).

FABRIC SELECTION,
DESIGN TECHNIQUES
AND
EQUIPMENT
REQUIREMENTS

Fabric Selection, Design Techniques, and Equipment Requirements

FABRIC SELECTION

Selecting fabric is a Pandora's box of challenge and exhilaration! Quilters are faced with an extensive supply of printed cottons, dyed batiks, woven brocades, ikat, stripes, and plaids. Many quilters use cotton cloth exclusively. Other fiber artists incorporate a range of textiles, fiber content, weaves, and textures in their designs. In most cases, the end use of the item—a quilt, garment, wallhanging—will determine the material selection and techniques incorporated in the piece.

FABRIC AND DESIGN
COLOR, CONTRAST, AND VISUAL TEXTURE

Studying photographs and observing items in daily life can be helpful when selecting fabrics, print scale, colors, and contrasting elements for your landscape.

You can use fabric patterns and designs to create design elements. In natural environments many principles apply.

OBJECTS IN THE FOREGROUND ARE LARGER IN SIZE AND MORE DISTINCT IN COLOR AND DETAIL.

LINES DECREASE IN WIDTH AS THEY RECEDE.

HORIZONTAL LINES CREATE A SENSE OF CALM.

VERTICAL LINES CREATE A SENSE OF DIRECTION AND HEIGHT.

BOTH NATURAL AND MANMADE ELEMENTS CREATE VISUAL INTEREST.

COLOR CHANGES IN SHADE AND HUE ON THE SAME
OBJECT, ACCORDING TO LIGHT AND SHADOW.

ZIGZAG LINES CREATE A SENSE OF ENERGY.

SOME PLANTS HAVE PROPORTIONALLY MORE FOLIAGE THAN FLOWERS.

OBJECTS DECREASE IN SIZE AND DETAIL IN THE DISTANCE.

CONTRASTING TEXTURES EXIST IN NATURE—SMOOTH, ROUGH, CURVED, LINEAR, FINE DETAIL, AND LARGE SCALE.

OBJECTS IN THE FOREGROUND ARE LARGER IN SIZE AND MORE DISTINCT IN COLOR AND DETAIL.

DIAGONAL LINES IN THE COMPOSITION CREATE INTEREST.

Selecting fabrics that emulate the desired visual effects can be challenging. Rarely are fabrics printed exactly like a photo. Therefore, it is important to select fabrics that have qualities that give an *impression* of the texture, light, shadow, tone, and hue.

Quiltmakers and textile artists may strive to replicate an image in every fine detail, or they may create a stylized design that is loosely based on the image. They artistically place printed and woven fabrics to represent the most important elements of the design. Stitched embellishments and quilting support and refine the textiles, blending the design into a complete composition.

Effective fabrics for landscape quilts are those that loosely replicate the theme of the design.

DETAIL OF *TETON RANGE* BY BETTIE RATNER (FULL QUILT ON PAGE 88). EFFECTIVE FABRIC SELECTION FOR THE MOUNTAINS, SKY, AND WATER.

MULTICOLORED FABRICS WITH DOTTY, FLOWERY, OR LEAFY SHAPES ARE EFFECTIVE IN THE FOREGROUND.

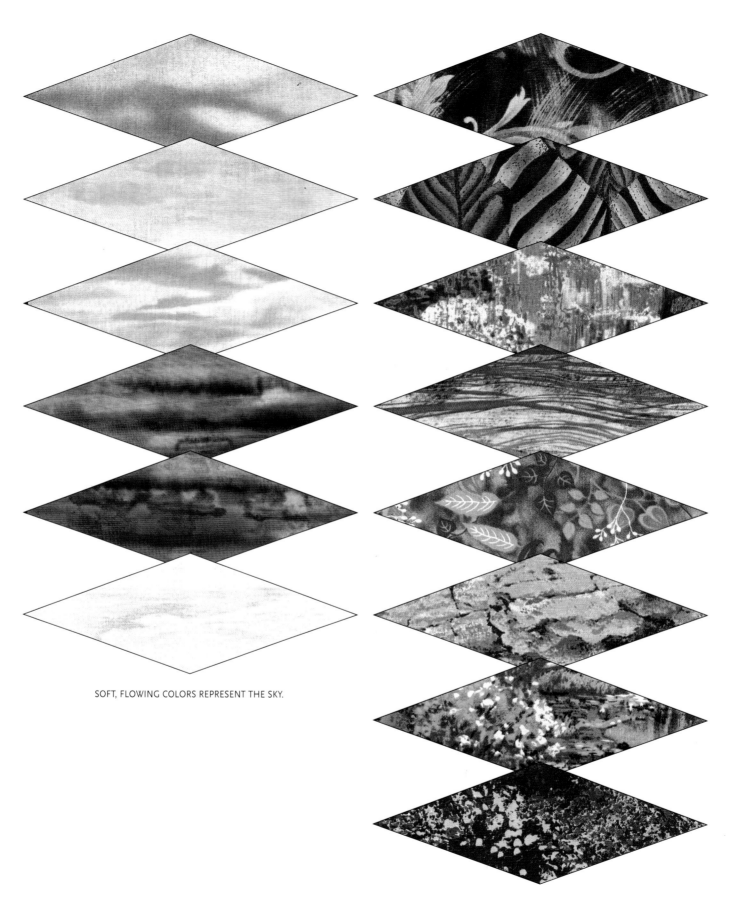

SOFT, FLOWING COLORS REPRESENT THE SKY.

MOTTLED, HAND-DYED, AND IRREGULARLY STRIPED FABRICS REPRESENT
PONDS, FOREST FLOORS, OR MIDRANGE LANDSCAPES.

DEEP, DARK SATURATED COLORS WORK WELL FOR SHADOWS.

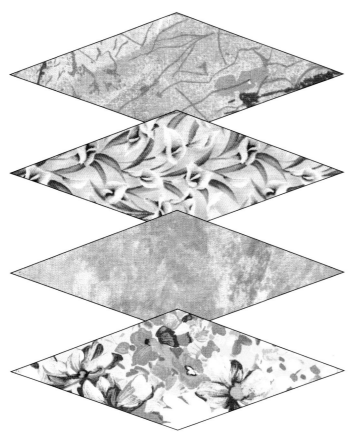

PATTERNS WITH STONES, BRICKS, AND TEXTURES ADD REALISTIC DETAIL.
USED PRIMARILY IN FORE- AND MID-GROUNDS.

BRIGHT COLORS OR PASTEL FABRICS ARE IDEAL FOR
HIGHLIGHTS AND BRILLIANT SUNLIT AREAS.

DESIGN TECHNIQUES

Pieced landscape designs may incorporate diamonds of different sizes in a beautiful flowing background that is simple to construct and visually appealing.

DIAMONDS OF VARIOUS SIZES CREATE AN INTERESTING BACKGROUND. DETAIL OF *MONTEREY PENINSULA* (FULL QUILT ON PAGE 82).

Expand the design theme with additional appliqué, stitching, and surface embellishment. Elements may be staged on the background, or the pieced design itself can incorporate the landscape or theme. For a naturalistic appearance, design elements should relate to one another in scale and perspective.

You can create this perspective by modifying the sizes and shapes of the objects. The following are different viewpoints:

♦ Bird's-eye, or overhead view (as if you were looking down from a bridge)

The flowers are fully open and symmetrical in shape, with a rounded center and petals radiating equally out from the center.

♦ Water- or ground-level view

Objects such as the flowers, buds, and lily pads shown here look different from the side. Note the growth from the base to the opened petals.

◆ Short- to medium-range vantage point

Create perspective by changing the size and shape of objects, such as the lily pads and flowers shown here. The appliqué shapes in the foreground will be larger and more distinct in detail. The distant objects will become smaller, less distinct.

◆ Long-range vantage point

Distant clusters of flowers, shrubs on the far shore, trees, bridges, and structures will be less distinct and more impressionistic. They are best rendered with snippets of cloth, spattery-style printed fabrics, or hand- or machine-embroidery stitches. Studying photography and paintings will reveal this principle and help you create more naturalistic compositions.

EQUIPMENT, MATERIALS, AND RESOURCES

DESIGN RESOURCES

♦ Photographs for inspiration: design files for your project (page 19)

♦ 1¼–4 yards felt, fleece, or flannel to create a design wall that will then be marked with a diamond grid (page 40) (If necessary, seam narrow pieces of fabric together to make a larger design surface.)

♦ Yardstick or long rotary ruler to mark design wall surface

OFFICE AND ART SUPPLIES

♦ Masking tape, transparent tape, glue stick

♦ Clear plastic page protectors or transparency sheets

♦ Fine and extra-fine permanent marking pens (used for marking the lines on the fabric design surface and template plastic)

SEWING AND CUTTING EQUIPMENT AND SUPPLIES

♦ Sewing machine feet: darning foot, ¼" foot, and walking foot

♦ Sewing machine needles: sharps, metallic, or embroidery topstitching

♦ Extra-fine .5mm glass-headed pins

♦ 200–300 safety pins (used to pin the diamonds to the background design surface, particularly if the design surface will be moved)

♦ Scissors: fabric and paper

♦ Seam ripper and thread snips

♦ Rotary cutting equipment: cutter, sharp blade, rulers, self-healing cutting mat

♦ Acrylic rulers: 3" x 18" and 6" x 24"

♦ Fussy Cutter 45° diamond guide (either 3" or 6½" size)

♦ Iron and ironing board

♦ Extra muslin or cotton duck for ironing surface

♦ Thread: a variety of sewing weight and decorative (for topstitching and quilting)

♦ Optional: flat storage trays for sorting diamonds
   Cardboard trays from canned goods
   Jelly-roll pans
   Cafeteria trays
   Disposable foil cookie pans

OPTIONAL EQUIPMENT

♦ Photocopier or overhead projector

♦ Light box

♦ Large sheets of paper for design layout

♦ Adhesive tape

MATERIALS FOR OPTIONAL SURFACE EMBELLISHMENT

♦ Template plastic

♦ Roxanne's Glue Baste-It or paper-backed fusible web adhesive

♦ Embroidery floss and needles for hand embellishment

♦ Decorative yarns, perle cotton, rope, string, or cord

♦ Beads, stones, shells, found objects

♦ Netting, tulle, or sheer fabrics

♦ Fabric cutouts for appliqué: leaves, flowers, stones, animals, and so on

♦ Water-soluble stabilizer film

♦ Tear-away stabilizer for machine appliqué

CONSTRUCTION
TECHNIQUES

Construction Techniques

You can use a variety of techniques to construct diamond landscape quilts. This versatility allows you to make original designs with your favorite construction methods, regardless of your skill level.

♦ Simple strip-pieced quilts from a variety of cotton fabrics create geometric designs ablaze with color. Two patterns, *Colorwash Lone Star* (page 117) and *Fruitful Harvest Placemats* (page 113) use pieced strip sets to create diamond yardage.

♦ Historic charm quilts feature single-template shapes (in our case, the 45° diamond), cut and pieced from a variety of fabrics into a whole design. *Monet Water Lily* (page 96) and *Colorwash Diamonds* (page 109) cover techniques for cutting and constructing diamonds in a charm quilt method.

Pictorial diamond landscapes are the most artistic and complex of the diamond quilts. The quilt components are laid out on a fabric grid, building an impressionistic scene. The background is pieced and a variety of design elements are added as appliqué, surface texture, or embellishment to enhance the theme. Several techniques for creating impressionistic diamond landscapes appear in the following chapter.

PREPARING THE DESIGN

To create an impressionist-style pictorial quilt, work from original photos, sketches, or your imagination. Incorporate your personal skills and artistry to create and enhance the design. Numerous design decisions are made *before* cutting your fabric, so *first* determine the following:

♦ Composition layers—background, midground, and foreground

♦ Areas of the design that will be pieced as the background

♦ Supplemental design elements that will be appliquéd, embellished, painted, or pieced will be *added on top* of the background

♦ Particular method(s) or technique(s) for constructing each layer—piecing, appliqué, embellishment, embroidery, quilted threadwork, beading, dyeing, painting, or stamping

TRACING DESIGN ELEMENTS FROM PHOTOS OR SKETCHES

Background

When working from a photo or a sketch, it is important to *simplify the design* and make it "sewable." Using a fine-tip permanent pen, trace the background areas onto clear transparency material. Remember that the background lies *behind* the design elements. If your design incorporates numerous appliqué or embellishment motifs in the foreground, the background can be simple. For example, if you are creating a garden, the background fabrics could be in various shades of green and brown. Optional design motifs, such as appliquéd flowers, shrubs, trees, wheelbarrows, birdbaths, or park benches, would overlap and obscure much of the background fabric.

Diamond-Grid Transparencies

Photocopy the different diamond grids on pages 59 and 60 onto overhead transparency sheets. Audition the transparent diamond grids on the photograph, turning the grid to orient the diamond rows horizontally and vertically. Determine the best design layout for your landscape or scene.

Place a diamond-grid transparency over the line-drawing transparency. Move the grid up, down, or twist it slightly left or right to change the angle of the diamonds (vertical, horizontal, angled) over the line drawing. You may need to enlarge or reduce the diamond grid to suit the image you are designing.

PHOTO BY JOHN STEWART

AUDITION DIFFERENT GRIDS ON THE SAME PHOTO TO SELECT THE BEST ORIENTATION AND SCALE.

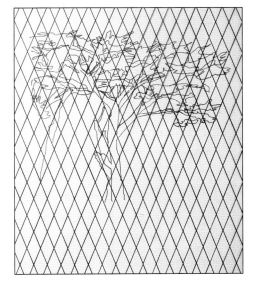

AUDITION DIFFERENT GRIDS ON THE SAME LINE DRAWING.

Test several diamond grids to get the best scale for rendering your design. Remember that a small-scale grid translates into more diamonds but will create a more interesting and detailed design. Select the most appropriate diamond-grid scale for your quilting skill level.

Mid- and Foreground Elements

Trace a variety of images from different sources to personalize and complete your design. In a garden quilt, for example, you might want to include favorite flower varieties that normally bloom in different seasons or to add a garden gazebo or sculpture to create interest. This is *your design*, and you can create the quilt of your dreams! I recommend that you use your own photography or sketches. If using commercial photography, remember to obtain the photographer's permission to avoid copyright infringement issues.

TRACE ELEMENTS FROM YOUR PHOTO ONTO CLEAR TRANSPARENCY MATERIAL.

CREATING A FULL-SIZED PATTERN USING AN OVERHEAD PROJECTOR

To enlarge the background design transparency using an overhead projector, tape a large piece of paper (or several smaller sheets, taped together) to the wall. Place the overhead projector on a small table and project the image onto the paper. Move the projector closer or farther away until the image is approximately the desired size. Trace the background design onto the paper. Pin diamond fabrics directly to the paper pattern until the surface is filled.

To add mid- and foreground designs to the quilt, it is necessary to determine their scale and placement on the background. This may be accomplished by various methods:

Project traced design elements onto the main pattern drawing, background grid, or pieced background. Move the projector, adjusting the size and position of the motifs until the image is the right scale. Pin a fresh piece of paper in place on the wall; trace the motif at the correct size. Use the traced image as a pattern to cut various fabrics for appliqué.

PLACE AN IMAGE TRANSPARENCY ON AN OVERHEAD PROJECTOR.

PROJECT THE IMAGE ONTO A LARGE PIECE OF PAPER. TRACE THE IMAGE(S) TO CREATE THE PATTERN.

ALTERNATE METHOD—CREATING A FULL-SIZED PATTERN USING A PHOTOCOPIER

If you do not have access to an overhead projector, take the traced image to a local photocopy shop. Make enlargements of the image until it is the desired size. Some printing or copy businesses own oversized copy machines. Keep in mind that these enlargements, although timesaving, can be expensive.

Next, make copies of the original photo with a transparent grid on it. You now have two images to reference—the original photo and a copy of the same photo with a diamond grid superimposed on top. The diamond-grid photo is helpful when selecting fabrics.

Photocopy the traced images at various sizes. Once you have found a size that works well, roughly cut around each image. Position the images on the background, moving and overlapping them until you are satisfied with the design. Tape, glue, or trace the images in the final design on the master pattern or pin to the flannel grid or pieced background. Use the photocopy as a pattern.

PHOTOCOPY TRACED IMAGES AT VARIOUS SIZES
TO OBTAIN THE SIZE THAT WORKS FOR YOU.

CUT OUT IMAGES. POSITION THEM ON THE DESIGN
SURFACE UNTIL YOU ARE SATISFIED WITH THEIR PLACEMENT.

ADDING DESIGN ELEMENTS WITH APPLIQUÉ

Collect printed fabrics with designs of various sizes. Cut out printed fabric motifs and add them to the quilt design with your favorite appliqué method—hand, machine, raw-edge, turned-edge, or fused and stitched.

CUT OUT PRINTED FABRIC MOTIFS FOR APPLIQUÉ.

Embroider, stencil, stamp, paint, or dye on fabric, ribbon, leather, or other materials. Attach the motifs to the quilt surface with machine stitching or embroidery.

DETAIL OF *CAROL'S CATS* BY LYNNE LICHTENSTERN (FULL QUILT ON PAGE 77)

DETAIL OF *RIVER RUN* BY CASSANDRA WILLIAMS
(FULL QUILT ON PAGES 78 AND 79)

DRAWING A GRID ON FLANNEL FOR A DESIGN SURFACE

The diamond grid drawn on flannel provides a surface on which you can hold and organize the design elements until the pieced background is assembled. (If you are working from a full-sized copy, the paper surface will serve as the design foundation; see page 38.) It is helpful to make the grid $\frac{1}{2}$" smaller than the cut size of the diamonds. Single diamonds will overlap at the edges, simulating the space taken up by seam allowances when pieced.

Method 1:

1. Position a 6" x 24" acrylic ruler upside down, aligned over the template on page 42. Using a permanent marking pen (such as an Identa-pen or Sharpie marker) and a second ruler, draw the two straight lines on the underside of the first ruler. Allow the ink to dry.

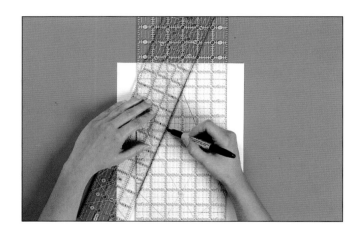

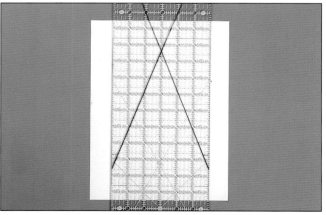

MARK BOTTOM OF RULER WITH 22.5° GUIDELINES.

2. Turn the ruler right side up. Align one of the pen lines against one edge of the flannel or fleece, establishing the angle of the grid. Measure the distance needed to make the finished diamonds of your project, and mark parallel lines in one direction across the fabric at the angle. Rotate the ruler, aligning the 45° guide line with one of the inked lines on the fabric. Mark parallel lines in the opposite direction, creating an entire surface with 45° diamonds.

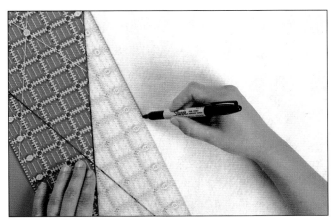

MARK DIAMONDS ON THE DESIGN SURFACE USING A MARKED RULER.

Method 2:

1. Copy the guide on page 42.

2. Pin the paper copy in the lower corner of the felt or fleece.

3. Align the edge of a 6" x 24" ruler alongside one guideline, establishing the angle of the grid. Draw a line. Begin drawing lines parallel to the first line the width of a *finished* row of diamonds (cut size minus ¹/₂" for seam allowance). Mark parallel lines in one direction across the fabric at the same angle. Remove the paper guide to mark the lines beneath it. Rotate the ruler, aligning the 45° guide with one of the inked lines on the fabric. Mark parallel lines in the opposite direction, creating an entire surface with 45° diamonds.

MARK DIAMONDS ON THE DESIGN SURFACE USING THE GUIDE.

JAN'S TIPS

Extend the length of a standard 6" x 24" ruler for easier marking. Carefully align and tape two rulers together, end to end, using clear packaging tape. Remove the tape after marking the grid lines.

Easily remove permanent ink from ruler surfaces with rubbing alcohol or a plastic eraser (no grit to scratch the surface). Never use a solvent of any kind, as it will also remove the ruler's printed lines!

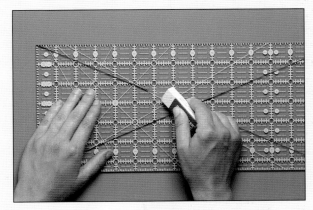

REMOVE PERMANENT INK LINES WITH AN ERASER.

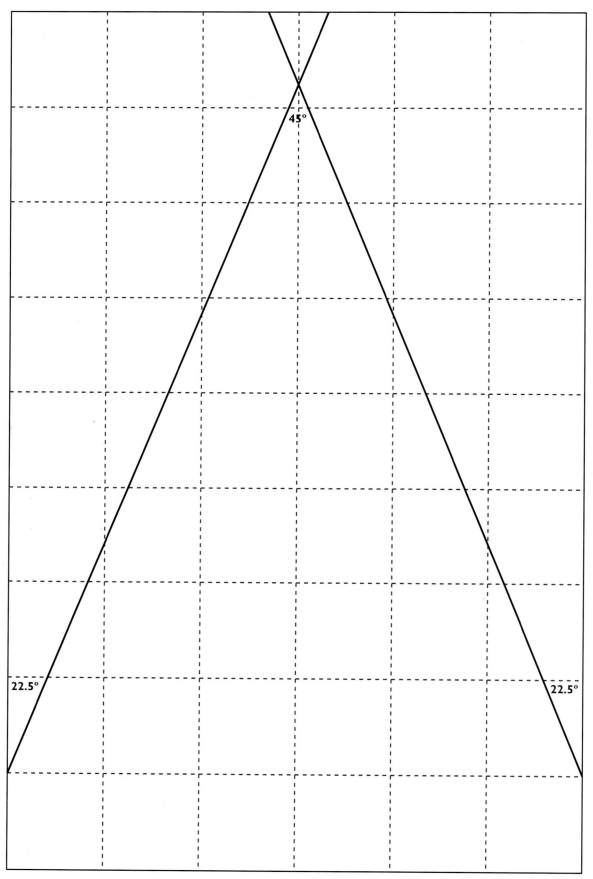

45°

22.5°   22.5°

22.5° GUIDE FOR MARKING THE BOTTOM SIDE OF AN ACRYLIC RULER

CUTTING THE FABRICS

FABRICS FOR THE DIAMOND BACKGROUND

Refer to pages 24–29 to choose fabrics for the diamond background.

CUTTING DIAMOND STRIPS AT A 22.5° ANGLE

Follow these instructions to cut a few diamonds from a variety of fabrics.

The diamond background is most stable when the woven grain line is horizontal and vertical in the final quilt top. Fold a 45° diamond in half, either tip to tip or across the shortest width (the "belly" of the diamond), and press a crease at each fold. Align the diamond's center folds with the grain on the fabric, either lengthwise or crosswise. The outer edges of the diamond will not fall on a straight grainline. The strips and subsequent diamonds must be cut at an angle to position the grainline correctly within the diamond shapes.

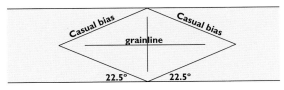

45° DIAMOND WITH GRAINLINE NOTATIONS—
EACH EDGE IS A CASUAL BIAS EDGE.

Exceptions include cutting scraps or fabrics with specific design motifs. This is known as *fussy cutting*. Fabrics are fussy cut individually to create diamonds with strategically placed design motifs. Note that the grainline may not line up in the center of the diamond for individual units.

Advance fabric preparation will result in ease of cutting and piecing. Mist any soft, loosely-woven, or prewashed fabrics with spray starch and press. The starch provides body so that the fabric will be somewhat stiff. Cut the fabrics into manageable lengths; 18" x 21" fat quarters (for cutting just a few diamonds from a large number of fabrics) or 18" x 42" half-yard cuts (for strip piecing with the same fabrics in greater quantities).

Sort precut diamonds into stacks by color and store on trays for easy use at the design wall. Cut additional diamonds as needed.

CUTTING WITH THE FUSSY CUTTER 45° DIAMOND GUIDE

The Fussy Cutter diamond guide (available from C&T Publishing) is a handy tool for cutting 45° diamonds from strips of fabric. The lines printed on the ruler, which also provide a 22.5° and a 67.5° angle, are used in conjunction with a standard long acrylic ruler when cutting strips. The diamond guide establishes an angle for the cut strip, determined by the grainline placement within a single diamond.

Stack several layers of fabrics *face up* for cutting. Align all stripes or directional prints with the *pattern oriented the same way*, even if the print is running lengthwise in one fabric and crosswise in another. Keep the directional fabrics on the top layer to ensure correct pattern placement when cutting the diamonds. Layer as many fabrics as you are comfortable cutting with your rotary cutter. A cutter with a sharp 45mm- or 60mm-diameter blade allows accurate cutting through multiple layers.

Lay the Fussy Cutter diamond ruler on the fabric. Orient the ruler so the printed pattern appears through the ruler in the way you prefer. Placement on allover patterns is not critical, but be deliberate when positioning the ruler to take best advantage of directional fabrics.

Make sure that the fabric edges are parallel to the ruler's centerline. Slide the diamond ruler to either edge of the fabric, aligning the edges with the ruler's centerline. The ruler remains at the same angle as when previewing the fabric pattern through it. Remember, the centerline should be placed on the grainline, with the fabric pattern placed at the direction it will appear in the finished diamond.

After placing the diamond ruler on the fabric stack, align the long ruler next to it. Begin cutting strips the desired width through all layers.

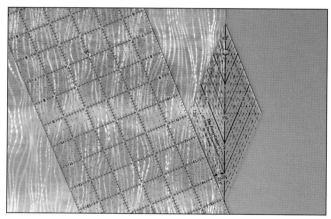

SLIDE THE DIAMOND GUIDE TO ONE PARALLEL EDGE AND ALIGN LONG ACRYLIC RULER NEXT TO IT.

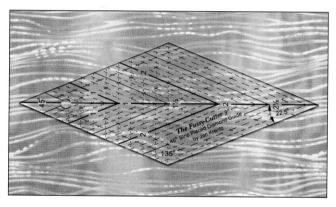

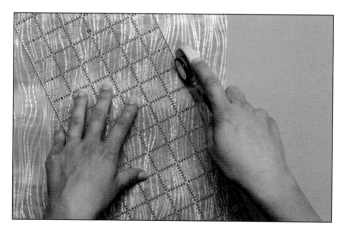

BEGIN CUTTING STRIPS AT ANGLE ESTABLISHED BY THE DIAMOND GUIDE. STRIPS' EDGES WILL BE CASUAL BIAS AND SLIGHTLY STRETCHY. HANDLE GENTLY TO AVOID STRETCHING.

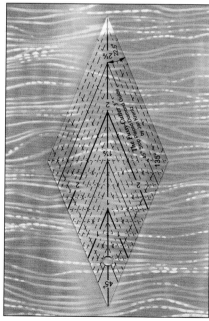

VIEW OF FABRIC PATTERN THROUGH THE FUSSY CUTTER DIAMOND GUIDE

Cutting With a Rotary Cutting Ruler

If you do not have a diamond ruler, mark the angles on the bottom of a long acrylic ruler with permanent ink to make a diamond guide (see page 40). Align the 22.5° guideline at the edge of the fabric stack. Begin cutting strips at this angle.

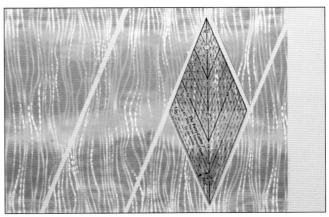

VIEW PRINTED PATTERN THROUGH DIAMOND GUIDE.
FABRIC PRINT DETERMINES PLACEMENT OF DIAMOND GUIDE.
CUT DIAMONDS SAME DIMENSION AS STRIP WIDTH.

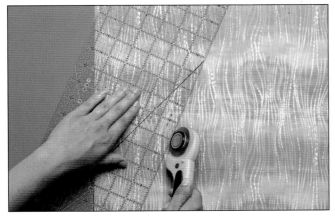

CUT FABRIC STACK AT ANGLE SHOWN.

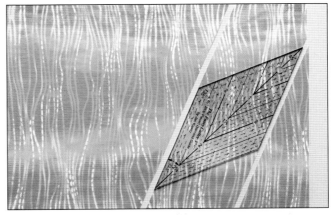

INCORRECT DIAMOND GUIDE PLACEMENT

Once the strips are cut, orient the diamond guide on a multilayered strip. View the printed pattern through the diamond guide, determining the angle the diamonds will be cut. The diamond guide may be turned, aligning one or another edge against the edge of the strip. *Pay attention to the angle of the guide to ensure that you are cutting the diamonds in the desired direction.* Cut diamonds the same dimension as the strip width. If you accidentally cut one stack of diamonds with the pattern or grainline in the wrong direction, stop, reorient the diamond guide, and continue cutting diamonds with the desired pattern alignment. Set aside or discard miscut diamonds.

PIECING THE DIAMOND BACKGROUND FROM INDIVIDUAL DIAMONDS

1. Arrange the fabric diamonds on the design surface, clustering areas of color together to follow your design. On the design surface, overlap the edges of the diamonds, approximating the reduced size when the seams are sewn. The size of the design will approximate the finished size following construction.

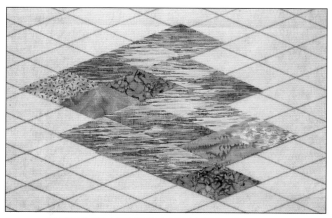

POSITION EACH DIAMOND AGAINST FOUNDATION GRID, ALIGNING SAME TWO EDGES AGAINST A GRID LINE. OVERLAP NEXT ROW OF DIAMONDS, SIMULATING AMOUNT OF FABRIC THAT WILL BE SEWN INTO SEAM ALLOWANCE.

2. Begin constructing individual rows of diamonds, working diagonally from one corner. (Follow my instructions on the next few pages to sew accurate ¼" seams and create perfect diamond intersections.)

CONSTRUCT DIAGONAL ROWS, WORKING FROM ONE CORNER.

3. Draw parallel lines on the cover of your ironing surface or use a pressing template (see Jan's Tip below) to press the diamond rows, taking care not to stretch or distort them. A mist of spray starch or fabric finish will help control distortion. If you used spray starch before cutting, simply moisten the strips with water to reactivate the starch in this step.

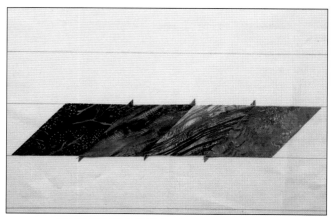

CREATE PRESSING TEMPLATE ON IRONING BOARD TO KEEP DIAMOND ROWS STRAIGHT AS YOU PRESS SEAMS.

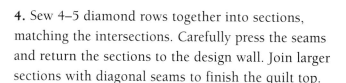

JAN'S TIP

To create a pressing template, use a permanent marker to draw parallel lines on a surplus piece of solid cotton cloth. Space the lines the width of your cut diamonds. Pin this cloth to the surface of your ironing board.

4. Sew 4–5 diamond rows together into sections, matching the intersections. Carefully press the seams and return the sections to the design wall. Join larger sections with diagonal seams to finish the quilt top.

SEWING AN ACCURATE QUARTER-INCH SEAM

Quiltmakers usually use ¼" seam allowances to piece their quilts. Rulers and rotary cutters allow us to cut very accurately, but I have discovered that there is a difference from one sewing machine to another and from one quiltmaker to another. Each quiltmaker's equipment, skill level, visual acuity, and many other factors can create slight variances. Complex pieced designs require more attention to accuracy, particularly seam allowances, so I routinely sew a couple of seam test units, making slight adjustments until my needle position and alignment against the presser foot result in an accurate scant ¼" seam allowance.

Anatomy of a Scant ¼" Seam Allowance

The seam allowance consists of the following:

♦ Two layers of fabric

♦ Stitched line of thread

♦ Fold of the fabrics being pressed open or to the side

The seam will actually be *one thread width narrower than ¼"*. It is more critical that the unit measures the correct size after the seams are stitched than that the seam width itself is correct. Thread diameter can also affect the width of the seam.

MAKING A TEST UNIT

1. Cut 3 strips of fabric, 1½" x 8". (You will want to choose 2 contrasting fabrics that also contrast with the color of the fabrics in your quilt so you can later use this test to make some templates for the 45° seam allowance; see page 50.)

2. Sew the 3 strips together using a ¼" seam allowance. Press the *seams open*.

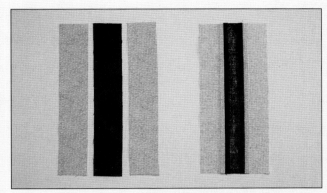

SEW 3 STRIPS OF FABRIC SIDE BY SIDE. PRESS THE SEAMS OPEN.

3. Measure the width of the unit. It should measure 3½" wide.

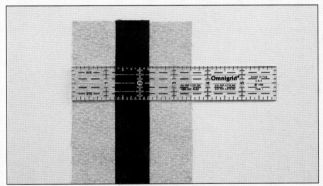

MEASURE THE WIDTH.

♦ If your piece measures 3⅜" wide, the seam allowance is *1 thread too wide*.

♦ If your piece measures 3⅝" wide, the seam allowance is *1 thread too narrow*.

Sew a new test piece, adjusting the seam accordingly (page 48).

Remember that the variance in seam allowance width is magnified *twice with each seam* (two fabrics in each seam) and multiplied by the number of seams sewn.

Adjusting Your Seam Allowance

Adjust your seam allowance in one of the following ways. You may need to make more than one correction.

Option 1

Move the needle position to the right or left of its current position. (This adjustment works only with machines that allow offsetting the needle right or left of center.)

Option 2

Purchase and use a ¼" presser foot manufactured for your sewing machine model. This is not a foolproof step because wider feed dogs for decorative stitching do not fully contact the narrow ¼" foot. Some ¼" presser feet may render a *full ¼" seam* rather than a *scant ¼" seam*. Use a seam test to determine the width. (Most ¼" presser feet allow you to move the needle one space to the right or left without the needle hitting the foot.)

Option 3

Change the alignment of the fabric edge to the presser foot. For example, if you currently align the fabric to the right outside edge of the presser foot, perhaps the fabric needs to be repositioned so it is hidden *beneath* the presser foot, and the alignment point is *in front of* the presser foot. Or you may need to position the fabric exactly *beneath* the presser foot, with no fabric visible at the edge of the presser foot.

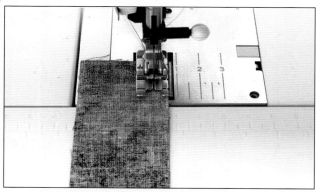

ALIGN FABRIC BENEATH THE PRESSER FOOT AT RIGHT EDGE.

Option 4

Position a small ruler with accurate markings beneath the presser foot. Lower the needle by hand until it touches the ruler, with the needle point just *inside* or *to the right of* the imprinted ¼" line. Align the ruler so it is square on the bed of the machine. Use a permanent marker to draw a line on the bed of the machine just ahead and slightly to the right of the presser foot.

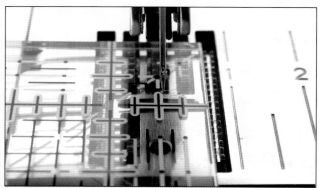

PLACE RULER BENEATH PRESSER FOOT AND LOWER NEEDLE BY HAND. NEEDLE SHOULD FALL TO RIGHT EDGE OF ¼" MARK ON RULER.

DRAW LINE ON BED OF MACHINE, FOLLOWING EDGE OF RULER.

Option 5

Rather than marking your machine, you can attach a 2½"-square acrylic ruler, a stack of painter's tape, moleskin, or any other rigid material in front of the presser foot. The raw edges of the fabric will butt smoothly against the raised edge of the attached guide, enabling you to position the fabric straight as it enters under the presser foot. Pins will ride over a low guide, or you can place the pinheads to the left when using a higher guide.

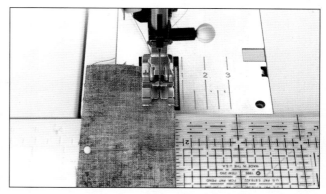
PINNING FROM THE LEFT WORKS WELL WITH A HIGHER GUIDE.

TAPE A SMALL RULER IN FRONT AND TO THE RIGHT OF PRESSER FOOT.

Option 6

Adjust the *rotary-cutting dimensions* to align the raw edge of the fabric to *include* the printed line in the total strip measurement (thereby increasing the strip width by one thread width).

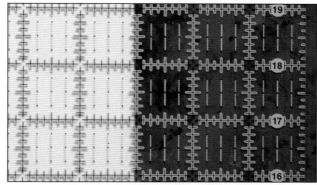
ALIGN RULER ON FABRIC LINE ON TOP OF FABRIC EDGE.

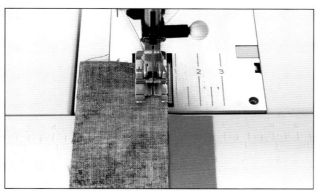
STACK SEVERAL LAYERS OF TAPE IN FRONT AND TO THE RIGHT OF PRESSER FOOT.

TECHNIQUE TOOLBOX

Routinely check the accuracy of your machine's seam allowance to discern any slight changes in needle alignment or seam width. Record machine settings in permanent marker on the seam test. Store seam-allowance tests with each quilt project so you can calibrate the seam allowance when returning to the quilt project after an absence.

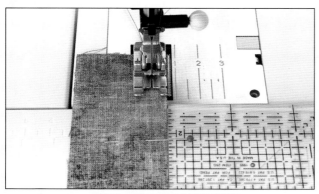
PINS WILL RIDE OVER A LOW GUIDE.

MAKING A 45° SEAM ALLOWANCE TEMPLATE

When you are satisfied with the accuracy of your seam allowance, here is a slick trick for creating a template to use while piecing the diamonds together.

1. Cut apart the seam-allowance test pieces parallel to the seam, as shown. (You will be cutting several test pieces so that you can eliminate some pieces if they are not accurate.)

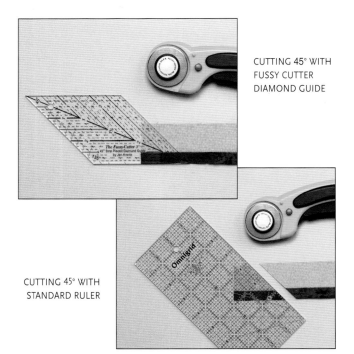

CUT SEAM-ALLOWANCE TEST PIECES APART, PARALLEL TO SEAMS.

2. Using the Fussy Cutter 45° diamond guide or an acrylic ruler angled at 45°, cut through the pieced seam sample at one end. Measure 1" from the first angled cut and make a second cut parallel to the first (also at a 45° angle).

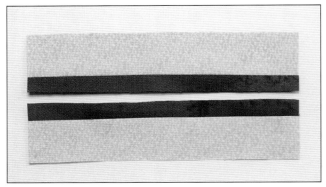

CUTTING 45° WITH FUSSY CUTTER DIAMOND GUIDE

CUTTING 45° WITH STANDARD RULER

CUT 1" FABRIC STRIPS PARALLEL TO FRESHLY CUT EDGE.

3. Fold a seam-allowance test piece with the right sides together, as shown. Use transparent adhesive tape to tape this test piece to the tabletop or the front of your sewing machine.

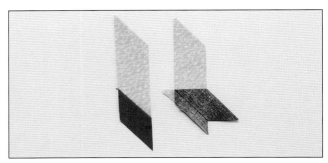

FOLD TEST PIECE RIGHT SIDES TOGETHER.

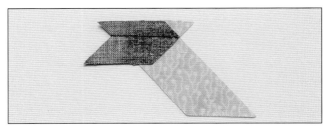

TAPE TEST PIECE NEAR YOUR SEWING MACHINE

A good seam sample features the following characteristics:
- Fabric edges that were aligned perfectly when sewn
- Distinct "dog ears" (¼" tips) visible at both ends
- Visible straight line of stitching that is representative of all the seams in the project
- No fold or pleat at the seam caused by poor pressing
- Seam-allowance test piece that contrasts in color with the surface where it will be taped for reference

SEWING TOGETHER INDIVIDUAL DIAMONDS USING A 45° SEAM ALLOWANCE TEMPLATE

Use the 45° seam allowance template to sew individual diamonds together with perfect seams.

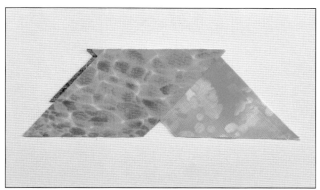

PLACE 2 INDIVIDUAL DIAMONDS RIGHT SIDES TOGETHER AND ALIGN THE ENDS, MATCHING THE $^1/_4$" OFFSET EXACTLY TO THE $^1/_4$" SEAM ALLOWANCE TEMPLATE. WHEN THE WHOLE ROW OF DIAMONDS IS ALIGNED PROPERLY, MATCHING INDIVIDUAL INTERSECTIONS BECOMES MUCH EASIER.

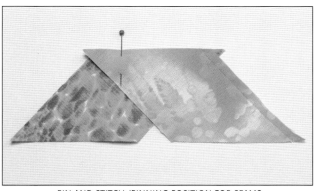

PIN AND STITCH (PINNING POSITION FOR SEAMS SEWN USING A LOW GUIDE, PAGE 49).

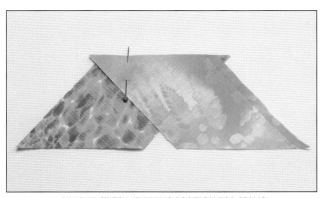

PIN AND STITCH (PINNING POSITION FOR SEAMS SEWN USING A HIGH GUIDE, PAGE 49).

Matching Seam Intersections

You can use a variety of methods to accurately align the diamond seams to create perfect intersections. The following methods all result in accurate intersections. Choose the one that works best for you. Some of the methods may work better for sewing individual diamonds together, and others are good for joining strip-pieced diamond strips.

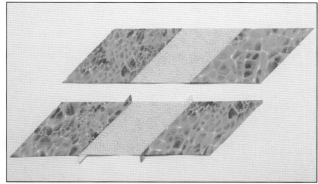

THE STRIP-PIECED DIAMOND STRIP (TOP) HAS NO DOG EARS; THE STRIP PIECED WITH INDIVIDUAL DIAMONDS (BOTTOM) HAS DOG EARS SHOWING.

Method 1

Positioning Pin

POSITION A SEAM TEST PIECE ON TOP OF THE 2 LAYERS OF STRIP-PIECED DIAMONDS THAT YOU ARE GOING TO SEW TOGETHER, ALIGNING THE DIAGONAL EDGE OF THE TEST PIECE WITH ONE SEAMLINE. NOTE THAT THE V-SHAPED CREVICE IS LOCATED AT THE LINE OF STITCHING. INSERT A PIN AT THE INSIDE POINT WHERE THE SEAM WILL BE SEWN.

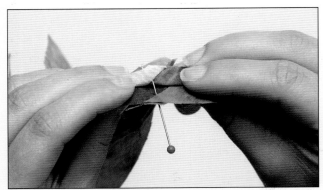

PUSH THE PIN THROUGH THE TOP LAYER. OPEN THE FABRICS TO SEE IF THE PIN PIERCES THE SEAM BENEATH AT EXACTLY THE SAME DEPTH.

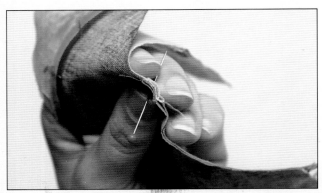

KEEP THE FIRST PIN VERTICAL. SUPPORT IT BY PLACING YOUR FINGERS ON EACH SIDE OF THE PIN, BENEATH THE FABRIC LAYERS.

INSERT A SINGLE PIN AT A SHALLOW ANGLE ON EACH SIDE OF THE VERTICAL PIN TO SECURE THE INTERSECTION. REMOVE FIRST (RED) PIN. STITCH.

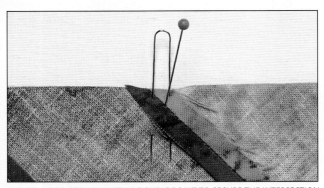

OPTION: USE A *FORK PIN* WITH A DOUBLE POINT TO SECURE THE INTERSECTION. REMOVE FIRST (RED) PIN. STITCH.

Method 2
Pinch and Peek

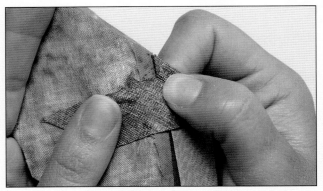

USE A SEAM TEST PIECE POSITIONED AT THE SEAMLINE.

PINCH WITH YOUR THUMBNAIL RIGHT AT OR BELOW THE LINE OF STITCHING ON THE TEST PIECE, HOLDING ALL LAYERS TOGETHER.

FLIP DOWN THE TOP SEAM ALLOWANCE AND PEEK INSIDE. THE 2 SEAMS SHOULD ALIGN. PIN TOGETHER TO SECURE. STITCH.

Method 3

Seam Offsets

The seams and seam allowances have a geometric relationship to one another. Offsetting them is the most accurate way to match intersections, but it takes some practice. Study this method and test it. Practice makes perfect!

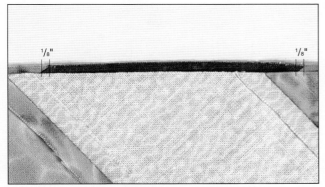

POSITION THE 2 DIAMOND STRIPS, RIGHT SIDES TOGETHER, WITH A SLIGHT GAP BETWEEN THE UPPER AND LOWER EDGES. ENVISION A SMALL GAP, APPROXIMATELY 1/8", BETWEEN THE LOWER SEAM AND THE CORNER OF THE UPPER SEAM ALLOWANCE.

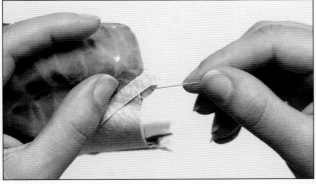

SLIDE THE LAYERS TOGETHER, MEETING THE IMAGINARY POINTS, AND PIN.

Method 4

Dot-to-Dot

If you have difficulty with any pinning method, try this technique. Remove the thread from the machine. Using a heavier-weight needle, prestitch the seam-lines without thread to perforate the fabric. Align the 2 layers, pinning directly from the top layer through to the second layer, using the perforations, or dots, as the guide.

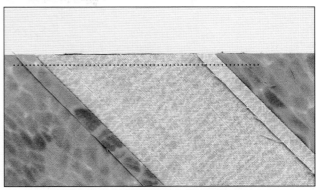

PRESTITCH THE SEAMLINE USING A HEAVIER-WEIGHT NEEDLE WITHOUT THREAD. ALIGN SEAM INTERSECTIONS, PINNING THROUGH THE HOLES ON BOTH LAYERS.

Method 5

Basting the Seam Intersections

You will have good results if you baste the intersections by machine. It is unnecessary to adjust the stitch length to a longer (basting) stitch.

STITCH JUST 3–4 STITCHES, SEWING SLOWLY AT EACH INTERSECTION. LIFT THE PRESSER FOOT AND TRAVEL TO THE NEXT INTERSECTION.

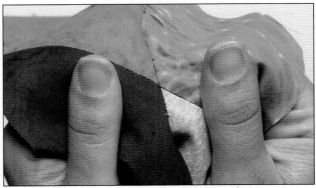

OPEN THE INTERSECTIONS TO CHECK ALIGNMENT. IF SATISFIED, SEW THE ENTIRE SEAM END TO END. IF THE POINTS ARE NOT ALIGNED, PULL JUST A FEW THREADS AND REALIGN THE INTERSECTIONS USING THE DOT-TO-DOT METHOD.

CONSTRUCTION TECHNIQUES

BORDERS

To determine the preferred border treatment for your quilt, consider the following options.

Option 1

Clean trim the edges with the rotary cutter and ruler, trimming away the irregular edges.

Option 2

Add a decorative border surrounding the design to frame the quilt.

Option 3

For a pieced border, count the number of border pieces required to fill in the ends of the design. (Note: The top and bottom shapes are different from the side shapes.) Cut the correct number of pieces (see page 112 for template patterns for the border of a quilt using 2½" finished diamonds). Sew the border pieces to the quilt top, adding a piece to the end of each row, setting pieces into the inside corners, and backstitching at the ¼" seam at both ends after sewing the rows together. Press the top and trim any irregular outside edges.

ADDING DESIGN ELEMENTS WITH APPLIQUÉ

A variety of appliqué techniques are suitable for adding design elements to the pieced diamond background.

FUSIBLE APPLIQUÉ

Tools

Appliqué pattern or design shapes
Paper-backed fusible web
Iron and ironing board
Fine-line permanent marker
Scissors
Optional equipment: light box, appliqué
  pressing sheet

Basic Technique

All design pieces: Place the fabric with the printed design or the pattern shapes wrong side up on a light box, or tape it to a window. Trace the *reversed* shapes onto the paper side of the fusible web. Roughly cut the shapes to be fused to different fabrics.

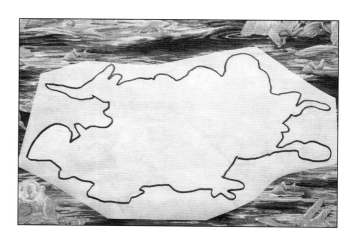

Small shapes: Use an iron to adhere the paper-backed fusible shapes to the wrong side of the fabrics. Cut out the shapes, peel away the paper backing, and place them on the quilt top. Press with an iron to adhere the shapes to the quilt top.

Large shapes: Cut away the *inner portion* of the fusible web, leaving approximately ¼" just inside the cutting line. Adhere the fusible web to the wrong side of the fabric. Cut out the design on the outline.

TRIM FUSIBLE WEB.

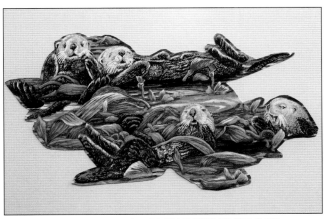

TRIMMED SHAPE READY TO BE ADHERED TO THE QUILT

Complex appliquéd elements: Place the line drawing or pattern beneath a translucent appliqué pressing sheet. Position the fusible elements, aligning them on the pressing sheet according to the design beneath. Press with an iron to adhere the layers together. Allow the appliqué motif to cool. Remove from the pressing sheet and position the motif on the quilt top. Press again with an iron, adhering the appliqué motif to the quilt top.

PLACE LINE DRAWING BENEATH APPLIQUÉ PRESSING SHEET, POSITION ELEMENTS ON TOP OF PRESSING SHEET, AND PRESS. COOL, REMOVE FROM PRESSING SHEET, AND POSITION.

Stitch all fused appliqué shapes to permanently attach them to the quilt top and to finish the raw edges. For stitching options, see page 57.

HAND OR MACHINE TURNED-EDGE APPLIQUÉ

Tools

Appliqué pattern
Template material (paper, plastic, or freezer paper)
Scissors
Pins
Chalk, lead, or colored pencils
Hand-sewing needles or sewing machine and a
   variety of colored thread to match appliqué fabric

Basic Technique

Create pattern pieces for each element in the appliqué design.

Cut out the pattern pieces *without a seam allowance* to create plain paper, plastic, or freezer-paper templates (see details on page 56).

Lightly trace the shape on the right side of the fabric, using a colored pencil or chalk pencil. Cut out the pattern pieces, adding a narrow $\frac{3}{16}$"–¼" seam allowance all around. Clip all inside corners to turn under the seam allowance easily.

OPTION 2: TRACE THE PATTERN PIECE ON THE RIGHT SIDE OF THE FABRIC. ADD A NARROW SEAM ALLOWANCE WHEN CUTTING.

Template Options

Option 1

Plain Paper Templates

Pin the paper template to the wrong side of the fabric. Turn the seam allowances over the paper and finger-press. Baste the seam allowances down with needle and thread.

Option 2

Plastic Templates

Hold a plastic template in place by hand on the right side of the fabric. Trace lightly around the outer edges with chalk or a colored pencil.

Option 3

Freezer-Paper Templates (used in two different methods)

Method 1 (paper on the right side)

Press the template to the *right side* of the fabric. Trace lightly around the shape and remove the freezer paper. Cut out, adding a seam allowance. With the needle-turn technique, turn seam allowances under by hand when stitching the shape to the background. Another option is to needle-turn the seam allowances under with the freezer paper in place. Remove the paper after stitching.

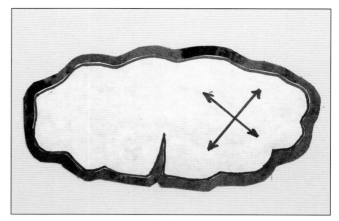

OPTION 3, METHOD 1: PRESS, TRACE, REMOVE PAPER.

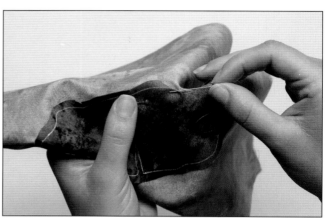

CUT OUT, NEEDLE-TURN, AND STITCH.

Method 2 (paper on the wrong side)

Press the template to the *wrong side* of the fabric. Trim the fabric, adding a seam allowance. Press the seam allowance under, using the freezer paper to shape the edge. You may add starch to moisten the edges before pressing. This results in a crisp, clean turned edge that remains flat for stitching. Remove the paper after pressing.

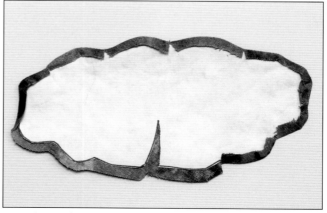

OPTION 3, METHOD 2: PRESS, TRIM, AND PRESS SEAMS UNDER.

APPLIQUÉ FINISHING OPTIONS

Here are some hand-finishing options.

◆ Buttonhole stitch

◆ Hidden appliqué stitches

◆ Embroidery stitches with decorative thread

DECORATIVE MACHINE STITCHING ENHANCES APPLIQUÉ DESIGNS ON *MY GARDEN* BY PATRICIA VOTRUBA (FULL QUILT ON PAGE 86).

STRAIGHT-STITCH, RAW-EDGE APPLIQUÉ FLOWERS AND LILY PADS ON *MONET WATER LILY* BY THE AUTHOR (FULL QUILT ON PAGE 98)

DETAIL OF HAND APPLIQUÉ FROM *GRAMPA'S BARN* BY PAM KAY (FULL QUILT ON PAGE 80)

Here are some machine-finishing options.

◆ Straight stitching

◆ Decorative stitching

◆ Satin stitching

APPLIQUÉ MOTIFS ON *KIMBERELY MYSTIQUE* BY GLORIA LOUGHMAN (FULL QUILT ON PAGE 94)

ADDITIONAL SURFACE TECHNIQUES

Embellishment options are numerous. Additional thread work, stenciling, dyeing, painting, embroidery, beading, sheer fabric overlays, attached trinkets and charms, photo transfers, snipped fabric collages, and other decorative techniques create design elements, small details, subtle shadows, and design highlights.

HAND-PAINTED LOBSTERS ADD DETAIL TO THE UNDERWATER SCENE IN *DANCE OF THE DEEP* BY CASSANDRA WILLIAMS (FULL QUILT ON PAGE 74 **AND** 75).

SMALL, DENSE FLOWER CANOPIES MAY BE RENDERED BY SNIPPING FABRICS INTO SMALL PIECES AND SEWING TO QUILT TOP.

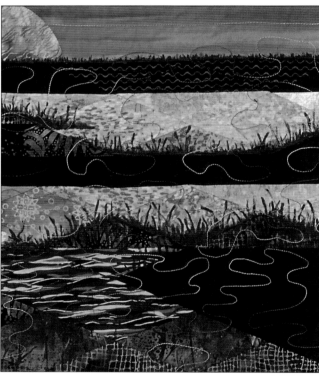

ALISON MORTON'S SNIPPED FABRIC COLLAGE ADDS REALISTIC TEXTURE TO *SPRINGTIME IN THE VALLEY* (FULL QUILT ON PAGE 83).

HAND-PAINTED GRASSES ADD DETAIL TO *THE WETLANDS* BY BETTIE RATNER (FULL QUILT ON PAGE 69).

COPY ONTO A CLEAR TRANSPARENCY PAGE AND TURN HORIZONTALLY OR VERTICALLY IN DESIGNING DIAMOND LANDSCAPES.

COPY ONTO A CLEAR TRANSPARENCY PAGE AND USE AS AN ALTERNATIVE TO THE GRID ON PAGE 59 IN DESIGNING DIAMOND LANDSCAPES.

chapter
4

GALLERY
OF
QUILTS

Monet's Pond at Sunset

by Betty Alofs
47" x 38"

This quilt started as a simple Monet's Pond quilt, but Betty didn't know when to quit! She added the bridge, branches with moss, and hanging flowers, and finally decided it was done.

THE WATERLILY POND BY CLAUDE MONET, 1896,
PHOTO 2004 MUSEUM OF FINE ARTS, BOSTON

Reflections

by Priscilla Bianchi

49" x 60"

Machine quilted by Laura Lee Fritz

This is a true scrap quilt, created using improvisational techniques with a focus on a spontaneous creative process. Hundreds of horizontal strips connect and break—only to connect again—to create movement and give the impression of a mirage reflecting water and sky. The complementary color scheme, rusts and turquoises, is a quilter's eye candy.

Foot Path to Todos Santos

by Priscilla Bianchi
43" x 55"

Machine quilted by Laura Lee Fritz

Inspiration for this design came from traditional textiles worn by the people of Todos Santos, a small town in Guatemala's mountainous highlands. In their costume, the vertical zigzag symbolizes the footpaths that people leave behind when they walk up and down the steep mountains. The block was inspired by Mary Mashuta's *Stripes in Quilts*.

Rain Forest

by Priscilla Bianchi
37" x 49"

"Greens of the forest, blues of the water . . . I can almost hear the rain falling and smell the wet earth." The blue zigzags were inspired by deep, rich Guatemalan textiles. Priscilla's creations start out as "dancing visions, designs, and colors" in her mind. Thus, this quilt is the labor of busy hands, a loving heart, and an innovative mind. It speaks of Priscilla and the pleasure she found in the quilt's making.

Hills Like White Elephants

by Edie Brown

56" x 41"

Hiking in the mountains of Nepal, crossing bridges throughout her life . . . Edie had enormous fun making this quilt! The materials include hand-dyed cottons and silks from a trip to Southeast Asia. The hand-dyed fabrics and embellishments were a joy for Edie to make. "Hills Like White Elephants," a short story by Hemingway, is only three pages long, yet the characters are fully developed. Similar to writing a short story, designing this quilt captured one of Edie's memories of growing up in Manitoba—a glimpse of dewdrops on leaves in the early morning sun. She wasn't sure where the design process was taking her, yet there was a sense of fullness when the quilt came together.

The Hills are Alive

by Suzanne Kistler

55" x 46"

In 1998, Suzanne's family vacationed in Whistler, British Columbia, Canada. Her daughter, Allison, was tired of posing for photos, so Suzanne suggested she sing the theme song from *The Sound of Music*. Allison also played a starring role in making the quilt. She was the one to draw her face and hand; Suzanne did the rest.

Pasture Eyes

by Suzanne Kistler

30" x 33"

Several years ago, Suzanne promised to make a "cow quilt" for her husband's secretary. The diamond landscape technique offered the perfect solution to creating a cute quilt in a timely manner.

Advent Calendar

by Suzanne Kistler

47" x 64"

For years, Suzanne had wanted to make an advent calendar, but inspiration escaped her. When she was introduced to the diamond landscape, the grid shouted, "Advent calendar!" The author's suggestions of buttons and ribbons to attach the ornaments were the perfect finishing touch. Suzanne loves this quilt.

The Wetlands
by Bettie Ratner
52" x 43"

A photo in an old book from the 1930s inspired this quilt. Some of the fabrics are tea-dyed with green tea. The sky is all one piece of fabric, and the cattails, reeds, and tree are painted details that unify the different areas in the design.

Tamsen Lake
by Jan Kolarov
71" x 58"

A photo of Tamsen Lake taken by Jan's sister inspired her quilt. It is a private lake near Donner Pass in the High Sierra, named after the daughter of one of the Donner brothers. It is machine pieced and appliquéd (also fused), with appliquéd and stitched plants.

Pond Life

by Patricia Richie
70" x 50"

The background colors were inspired by a photo of a pond scene. Once that was completed, Patricia started the foreground embellishments with the white egret, which was machine appliquéd. Patricia sought design inspiration from the pond environment. The dragonflies, frogs, caterpillar, and tree moss were free-motion machine embroidered. The tree, cattails, lily pads, and flowers (courtesy of the author) were machine appliquéd to the background, which was also part of the quilting.

Raging Fire-River Sanctuary

by Patricia Richie

58" x 48"

The summer of 2000 brought devastating fires to the Bitterroot Valley of western Montana. A photo of elk seeking refuge in the river with fire blazing all around was the inspiration for this piece. The background was pieced to resemble the fires and the river, and the elk were free-motion embroidered and then appliquéd to the piece during the quilting process. The piece was heavily quilted, including trees, flames, brush, and other details.

Memories of Africa

by Sandra Wagner

51" x 39"

The grandeur of Africa was so powerful that sounds and smells still trigger memories that Sandra will never forget. Visiting the zoo will never be the same again.

Dance of the Deep

by Cassandra Williams

68" x 53"

Hand-painted fish and sea anemones add
detail to this wonderful underwater scene.

Frolic

by Mona Baran
42" x 40"

Frolic was inspired by a coloring book Mona found at a quilt show. The diamonds create a whimsical garden background for the fairies' play.

Carol's Cats

by Lynne Lichtenstern
38" x 52"

A friend whose family was adopted by several cats commissioned this quilt. The quilt is a garden scene, featuring all of the family cats throughout time. Cotton fabrics, machine piecing, machine appliqué, and quilting come together in this quilt.

River Run

by Cassandra Williams
69" x 37"

In Oregon, the fishermen in Cassandra's family thrill to see the seasonal run of spawning salmon and trout. Now her fisherman can see them run year-round.

Chromatic Spectrum, Roy G. Biv

by Kathy Butler
40" x 31"

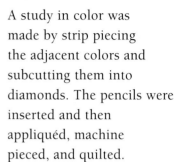

A study in color was made by strip piecing the adjacent colors and subcutting them into diamonds. The pencils were inserted and then appliquéd, machine pieced, and quilted.

Grampa's Barn

by Pam Kay
48" x 34"

The barn in this quilt looks just like the one in rural Medford, Minnesota, where Pam's Grandpa Guimond raised pigs. What a sweet memory it is for her.

Machine quilted by D'Andrea Mitchell

Aurora Sentinel

by Jacqué J. Holmes
56" x 48"

Machine quilted by Charlotte Freeman

Jacqué's fascination with the aurora borealis led to this quilt. She has also become enamored with the stately moose. Although the placement of the colors in the aurora was very time consuming, she enjoyed the design of the trees and the moose silhouettes. Finally, the machine quilting by Charlotte Freeman added the absolute finishing touch.

Monterey Peninsula

by Jan Krentz

65" x 51"

The Monterey Peninsula is an area rich in vegetation, mammals, and sea life.
Design elements include a whale, sea otters, a cypress tree, California poppies,
quail, fuchsia ice plant, and blue lupine. The background is pieced and hand
painted; embellishments are painted, stamped, stenciled, cut from printed fabric,
and machine and hand appliquéd.

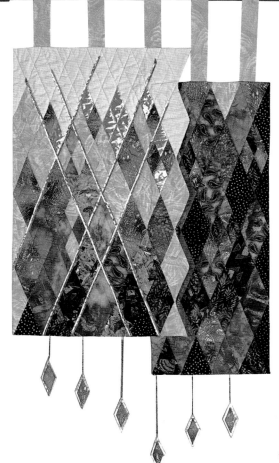

Diamonds Galore

by Carol Coor-Pender McCrea
23" x 43"

Carol designed and made this quilt expressly for the 2003 California-Australian Challenge. It is machine pieced and hand and machine quilted. *Diamonds Galore* was one of seven pictured in *Australian Quilters Companion*, #8.

Springtime in the Valley

by Alison Morton
69" x 60"

This quilt was inspired by the peach trees, that bloom so beautifully in spring in the San Joaquin Valley of California. The trees were made by cutting fabric into itty-bitty pieces, which were sprinkled onto water-soluble stabilizer in the rough shape of a tree. Alison sewed over every inch of the tree foliage, securing all of the little pieces. The finished trees were soaked in water to dissolve the stabilizer, air dried, and sewn onto the diamond background.

Tranquility

by Toni Silvera

51" x 72"

Machine quilted by T. G. Custom Quilting

Toni had this quilt in her head for many years before actually creating it. It did not turn out the way she had envisioned it, but she still loves it. The quilt is dedicated to two special people, her niece and nephew, Cassandra and Gary Silva. They have both inspired Toni and have given her direction. She is very proud of them and loves them dearly.

Sentinel of the Ages

by Kathryn Veltkamp

62" x 41"

The tree quilt was inspired by a photo taken by Kathryn's mother, Marge Van Wyk, in Canyonlands, Utah. Her mother submitted it to a photo contest and won a small space in a publication (retaining copyrights to the photo). She then painted a watercolor of the photo, and Kathryn created the quilt, using diamonds to construct the background. She designed the tree using appliqué, with extra batting behind the trunk and snips of various greens for the foliage. The quilt is free-motion quilted using variegated threads.

My Garden

by Patricia Votruba

51" x 29"

My Garden was inspired by Patricia's view of her garden outside her back door and the six fruits of the Bible. The fruits are appliquéd onto the diamond background and enhanced with decorative threads. Quilting designs vary throughout the piece according to the scene or the fruit near it—leafy in the trees, horizontal stitching in the sky, curly patterns in the vine areas, and so on. Patricia enjoyed the transition from one location to another and playing with the machine's free motion.

Ribbons of Spring

by Patricia Votruba

22" x 23"

The quilt features appliquéd spring flowers surrounded by a "window frame" of springtime-colored ribbons, which are crisscrossed in a diamond pattern. Machine-quilted floral stitches outline the ribbons and free-motion stitching is used in the background.

We Have Seen His Star...
Wise Men Still Seek Him

by Suzanne Kistler

44" x 65"

The Lone Star was pieced by adapting the author's Lone Star instructions. The star alone seemed to be missing something . . . a ray of light, perhaps? After piecing several diamond landscapes, aha! This technique is perfect to send the star's light to the sleepy world below.

If Melrose Had Glass

by Suzanne Kistler

35" x 48"

In 1996, Suzanne's family vacation included a visit to Melrose Abbey in Scotland. The window frames were still in place, although somewhat broken. Imagine what they would have looked like had the glass still been in place.

Teton Range

by Bettie Ratner

58" x 40"

Working from a photo of the Grand Teton mountain range, Bettie used an assortment of fabrics for the peaks. She maintained an angular orientation of the fabrics for more realistic mountains. The tree in the foreground is appliquéd over the top of the quilt, and the back is cut away. The fabrics are cottons; the quilt is hand appliquéd, machine pieced, and machine quilted.

Roger Ball

by Mary Beth Craig

52" x 33"

Mary Beth's husband, a Navy pilot, has taken many photos over the years he has served. Based on one of those photos, Mary Beth created this version of a F/A-18 Hornet as it approached the aircraft carrier. "Roger Ball" is the expression radioed by the landing signal officer to the pilot as he prepares to come aboard for an arrested carrier landing.

Botanical Magnolia Stellata

by Kathy Butler

46" x 38"

As a gardener, Kathy has always loved flowers and their appearance in art. She has a particular interest in botanical prints. The offset pieced background gives the appearance of old paper and the gold binding provides a frame. Her son, Jeff Farley, drew the magnolia blossom for her. The quilt is machine pieced, appliquéd, and quilted.

Reflections from Swan Lake

by Mary Beth Craig

52" x 34"

This quilt is a reminder of the many ballet performances Mary Beth's family has enjoyed, complete with curtains and dance floor. It is machine pieced, appliquéd, and quilted.

Kimberely Mystique

by Gloria Loughman

79 ½" x 84 ½"

The Australian Kimberely shelters one of the world's most amazing wilderness areas, and the challenge of traveling to this remote land is rewarded with the sight of the mystical boab trees. Gloria machine pieced, appliquéd, embroidered, and quilted hand-painted cotton and silk, hand-dyed fabrics, and batiks.

Colorwash Lone Star

by Kathryn Veltkamp

29" x 29"

Kathryn selected a rich floral collection for this pair of quilts (here and page 123). She enjoyed making both stars with the same fabrics. A skilled quiltmaker, Kathryn says both designs were fun to sew and look beautiful in her home. These quilts will be treasured gifts for family and friends. *Photo by Melinda C. Holden.*

Autumn Sunset

by Jude Ferris

30 ½" x 30 ½"

As the fabrics came together in this little quilt, Judith was reminded of the beautiful colors of an autumn sunset just before night overtakes the land. *Photo by Melinda C. Holden*

Monet Water Lily

by Jan Krentz

48" x 30"

Quilted by Carolyn Reynolds

Create a wallhanging reminiscent of impressionist artist Claude Monet's water lily paintings. Compose a "textile painting" with a collection of fabric diamonds and embellish with dimensional water-lily pads, flowers, and buds.

Research Claude Monet on the Internet or at the local library for design inspiration. Photographic images will be especially helpful when selecting color families for your project.

DETAIL, WATER LILY PAINTING
BY CLAUDE MONET

WATER LILIES BY CLAUDE MONET, 1906,
PHOTO 2004 MUSEUM OF FINE ARTS, BOSTON

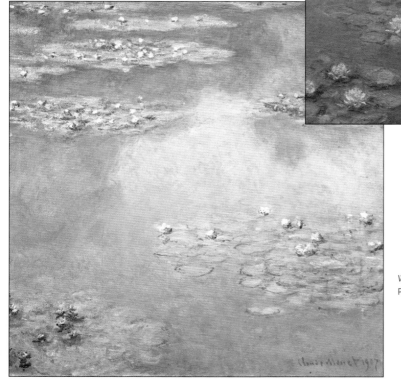

WATER LILY POOL BY CLAUDE MONET, CIRCA 1900,
PHOTO 2004 MUSEUM OF FINE ARTS, BOSTON

FABRIC SELECTION

Monet's color palette is broad and exciting. Studying his impressionistic paintings reveals a full range of colors. The water's surface reflects the sky and surrounding landscape, which change colors throughout the day and season. Select the colors you are most comfortable working with. You do not need to incorporate all of the color families in your composition.

SELECT FABRICS WITH CHARACTERISTICS SUITABLE FOR POND WATER, REFLECTED SKY, AND FOLIAGE.

MEDIUM TO DARK SHADES OF FABRIC TO REPRESENT THE REFLECTION OF FOLIAGE AND SHADOWS.

USE LIGHT TO MEDIUM SHADES FOR HIGHLIGHTS, REFLECTED SUNRISE, CLOUDS, MIDDAY SUN, OR SUNSET.

SELECT FABRICS WITH CHARACTERISTICS SUITABLE FOR POND WATER, SHADOWS, AND FLOWERS.

FABRIC REQUIREMENTS AND SUPPLIES

Supply list (See page 33.)

¼-yard pieces, fat quarters, or scraps (measuring at least 4" x 9") of 20–30 textural fabrics to total approximately 5–5 ½ yards. Select fabrics of varying colors (refer to Fabric Selection, page 98).

4–6 scraps (measuring at least 5" x 5") in several shades of the same color for flowers. Select opaque cotton for the stronger colors and sheer organdy, batiste, organza, or ribbon for the surface petals.

3–4 quarter-yard pieces or 10–12 scraps (measuring at least 7" x 7") of various fabrics for the lily pads. Select fabric colors that will coordinate with the pieced background yet that have enough contrast to be visible.

3–4 quarter-yard pieces or 10–12 scraps (measuring at least 8 ½" x 8 ½") for lily pad shadows and highlights. Select fabrics that will sharply contrast with both the lily pads and the background.

Backing: 1 ½ yards
Batting: 52" x 34"
Binding: ⅜ yard

Thread: variety of colors for decorative stitching
6mm glass foil-lined beads, "e" beads, or other beads with a large hole for the flower stamen

#5-weight perle cotton or crochet thread: a variety of colors for the flower stamens

Template plastic or freezer paper for appliqué templates

Water-soluble fabric glue, such as Roxanne's Glue Baste-It, for appliqué shapes

Paper-backed fusible web: 1–1 ½ yards for appliqué shapes (optional)

Water soluble stabilizer: 1 yard for stitching edges of appliqué shapes (optional)

NOTIONS AND EMBELLISHMENT ITEMS FOR WATER LILY QUILT

PREPARATION

1. Draw the diagonal grid lines 2½" apart on the felt, flannel, or fleece (see page 40). Use the background grid on page 108 as your guide for the number of rows needed. Mount the design surface on a vertical surface.

2. Cut three to five 3" diamonds each from a variety of fabrics. Sort the diamonds into stacks by color and store on trays or cardboard boxes for easy use at the design wall (see page 43). Cut additional diamonds as needed. The quilt uses approximately 180–200 diamonds.

3. Arrange the diamonds on the fleece, clustering areas of color together to create areas of sunshine, shade, foliage, or water in the composition. Repeat some of the fabrics in each area to create design flow. Overlap the edges of the diamonds on the design surface, approximating the reduced size once seams are sewn. The size of the design layout will approximate the finished size following construction.

CREATE AREAS OF LIGHT AND SHADE.

4. View the design surface intermittently from a distance to survey the composition as you work. This design evaluation may take as long as the other steps—don't rush the process.

CONTINUE PLACING DIAMONDS TO FINISH THE BACKGROUND DESIGN.

5. Create a ¼" seam template (see page 50). Tape it in front of you at the sewing machine for easy reference.

6. Begin constructing individual rows of diamonds, working diagonally from one corner into the body of the quilt. Press the seams open or to the side as you construct each row, and return it to the correct position on the design wall.

7. Press the diamond rows as described on page 46, being careful not to stretch or distort them. Construct sections of 4–5 diamond rows, matching the intersections. Carefully press the seams and return the sections to the design wall.

Optional: Offset the diamond rows, deliberately mismatching the seams to create a more organic appearance.

DIAMOND ROWS MAY BE DELIBERATELY OFFSET
FOR A MORE ORGANIC DESIGN.

8. Join the diagonal sections together, working from the corners toward the center. The final seam will join 2 halves into the whole quilt top.

9. Press the quilt top carefully, without distortion. Move the iron in the direction of the fabric's woven grain. Block the top into shape if it has become skewed.

10. Layer the pieced background composition of diamonds with batting and backing. Securely pin all 3 layers together. Machine quilt. The flowers and lily pads will be attached after quilting.

11. Clean trim the edges with the rotary cutter and ruler, straightening the edges and squaring the corners. Opposing sides should measure the same dimensions. Attach binding.

ASSEMBLING THE LILY PADS AND FLOWERS

The perspective of the lily pads will determine the size and shape of the appliqué shapes you will add to your composition (pages 30–31). The shapes in the foreground will be larger and more distinct, and the lily pads will have a rounded, oval appearance. The distant flowers and lily pads will become smaller, less distinct, and more flattened in appearance.

1. Trace the lily pads and flower petals (pages 107–108) onto template plastic or freezer paper. Feel free to create lily pads and flowers of different sizes to represent the perspective you desire. Cut out the templates with scissors.

2. If you are using fusible web, trace the lily pads onto the paper side of the fusible web, cut away the inner portion of the web, and adhere web to the wrong side of various colors of fabric (pages 54–55). You may want to reverse some of the lily pads. If you are using water-soluble fabric glue, trace the lily pads directly onto the various fabrics. Lily pads are not necessarily green! It is more important that the lily pad *contrasts* in color with the background where it will be placed. Cut out the lily pads.

3. Place the lily pads on a piece of contrasting color fabric, making sure the lower fabric shows beyond the lily pad. The contrasting fabric can be darker, to create shadow, or lighter, to create highlight.

CUT LILY PADS OF VARIOUS SHAPES AND COLORS.

THE LILY PADS SHOULD CONTRAST WITH THE BACKGROUND FABRIC.

4. Fuse the lily pad to the contrasting fabric. If you are using fabric glue rather than fusible web, run a very fine bead of Roxanne's Glue Baste-It under the lower edge of the lily pad and its slit. Glue the lily pad to the second fabric.

GLUE OR FUSE THE LILY PAD TO THE CONTRASTING SHADOW OR HIGHLIGHT FABRIC.

NOTE: You may prefer to turn the edges under and appliqué the lily pad to the quilt top using traditional appliqué methods.

5. Trim the lily pad shadow or highlight about ⅛" from the edge of the lily pad, *only along 1 edge*. (A natural shadow or highlight would not outline or surround the entire shape like a halo.)

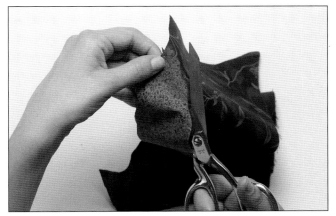

TRIM THE SHADOW OR HIGHLIGHT FABRIC.

6. Topstitch or appliqué the lily pad to the background, using coordinating or contrasting thread. Stitch the back (upper) edge of the lily pad to the quilt, using free-motion techniques with the darning foot about 1/16" from the raw edges. Leave the lower edge of the crevice unstitched so you can tuck the petals inside.

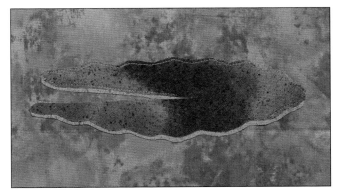

STITCH ALONG UPPER EDGES ONLY.

7. To make the flower petals, stack several layers of the cotton flower fabric together, one layer of each color. Trace and cut the flower petals using the templates or free-hand cut ovoid shapes from the flower colors with sharp scissors or a rotary cutter. The petal shapes should vary in size—some wider, some narrower, some longer, some shorter. To reduce raveling, cut the shapes so the bias grain falls along the outside edges of the petals.

ORIENT EDGES OF PETALS ALONG BIAS OF FABRIC.

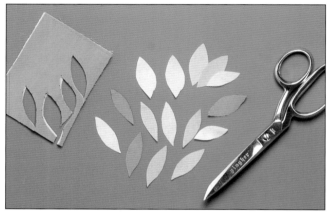

CUT PETALS OF VARIOUS SIZES AND SHADES OF SAME COLOR. EDGES SHOULD BE BIAS TO CONTROL EXCESSIVE RAVELING OF FLOWER PETALS.

8. Lay out a base layer of petals—approximately 4–6. (It's good to have some clusters with more petals and some with fewer petals, to replicate the flowers at different stages of bloom.) Cluster the base tips at the lily pad; the upper tips of the petals will fan out in a semicircle.

CREATE A BASE LAYER USING VARIOUS COLORED PETALS.

9. Glue-baste the petals in place. With your machine, topstitch the petals (free-motion with a darning foot) in an outline format, about $\frac{1}{16}$" from the raw edges.

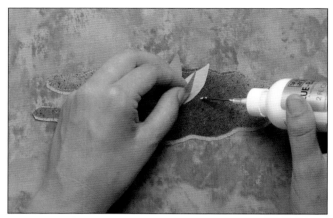

USE A VERY FINE LINE OF WATER-SOLUBLE FABRIC GLUE TO SECURE PETALS TO LILY PAD AND QUILT TOP.

RAW-EDGE APPLIQUÉ: STITCH PETALS TO BACKGROUND WITH FREE-MOTION STRAIGHT STITCH.

OPTION: STITCHED-EDGE APPLIQUÉ: STITCH PETALS TO BACKGROUND WITH BUTTONHOLE STITCH.

10. Thread a glass bead on a 6"–7" strand of #5 perle cotton. Twist the ends of the pearl cotton in opposite directions, creating a tight twist. To form stamens, allow the cord to wind up, twisting onto itself, with the bead at the tip. Make an assortment of colors—about 6–8 per flower. Adjust the number according to the fullness of the flower blossom.

NOTE: Select beads with larger holes; 6mm foil-lined beads are shown, but other styles of beads will also work nicely.

IF BEAD DOES NOT STAY IN MIDDLE OF FLOSS, HAVE A FRIEND HOLD BEAD AND PULL IT TO CENTER. BEGIN TO RELEASE TENSION ON FLOSS, ALLOWING TWIST TO BEGIN. RELEASE BEAD, AND IT WILL TWIST INTO STAMEN SHAPE.

THREAD A BEAD ONTO A STRAND OF PERLE COTTON FLOSS. TWIST FLOSS TIGHTLY IN OPPOSITE DIRECTIONS.

11. Cluster a group of stamens in the center of each flower clump. Pin, glue baste, or stitch them at the base to hold them in place.

CLUSTER STAMENS ON FLOWER BASE, AND PIN, GLUE, OR BASTE AT BASE OF STAMENS TO HOLD IN PLACE.

12. Cut another group of ovoid shapes from sheer and iridescent specialty fabrics of various shades. These are the front petals. Again, cut them so the bias grain falls on the longest edges to control raveling.

SLOWLY BRING ENDS OF FLOSS TOWARD ONE ANOTHER, ALLOWING IT TO TWIST UP ON ITSELF WITH BEAD AT TIP.

13. Position the sheer petals in front of the petal-and-stamen collections, adjusting the positions so they look natural.

POSITION SHEER PETALS OVER STAMENS.
USE FEWER SHEER PETALS FOR GREATER VISUAL EFFECT.

14. Free-motion straight stitch the petals with a small loop-shaped line of stitching, catching all of the threads, perle cotton, and petals to the surface. If you allow the upper tips of the front petals to remain free, they will tilt forward, as natural flower petals would do. You may need to tack the stamens (beads) into place if they tend to flop down. No batting is necessary to create a "stuffed" appearance beneath the lily pad or flower petals.

15. Stitch the remaining edges of the lily pad and shadow or highlight.

FREE-MOTION STRAIGHT STITCH, CATCHING ABOUT HALF OF PETAL, TO FORM LOOP OR TEARDROP SHAPES ON EACH PETAL.

Optional: Use a variety of decorative edge stitches, such as satin stitching, on the lily pads and petals.

Lay several flower petals on a single layer of water-soluble stabilizer film. Cover the petals with a second layer of stabilizer. Pin the layers to control all the pieces. Satin-stitch (fine zigzag) the outer edges of each petal. Soak the stabilized petals in water to dissolve the stabilizer. Dry the petals and appliqué them to the quilt.

OPTION: FLOWER PETALS WITH SATIN-STITCHED EDGING

JAN'S NOTE

The machine appliqué adds design dimension. I incorporate a variety of techniques and enjoy the appearance of raw-edge appliqué. The slight fraying causes the edges to appear organic and "meld" with the background. Trim any long threads that fray from the raw edges. Do not trim too closely, as the softly frayed edge is necessary to keep the pieces sewn to the quilt's surface.

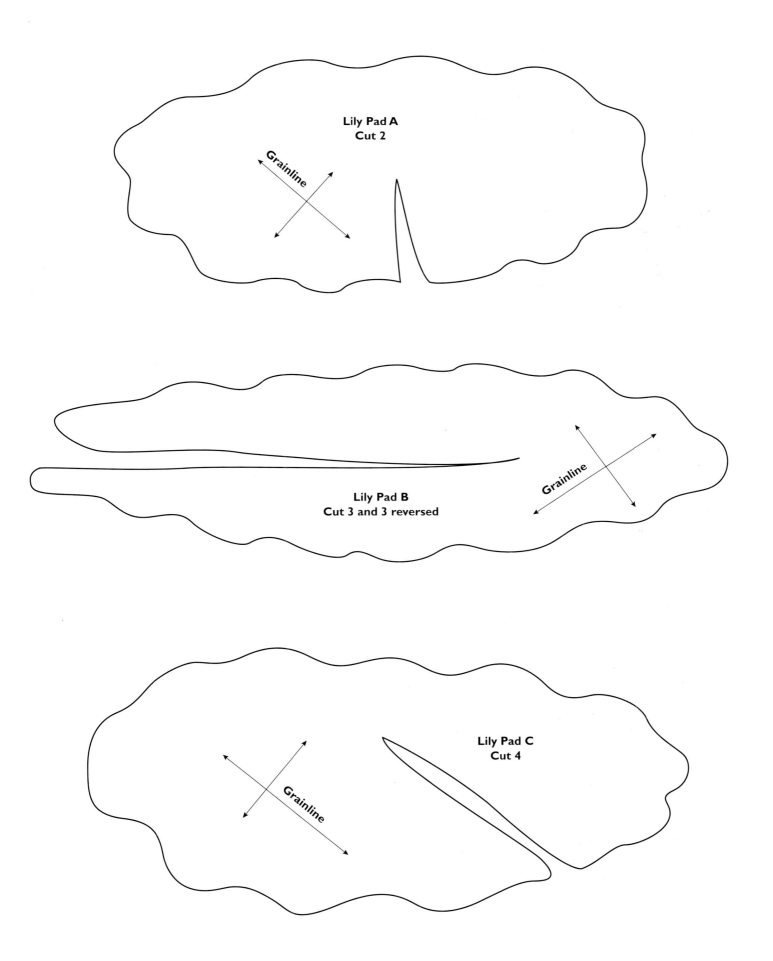

Lily Pad A
Cut 2

Grainline

Lily Pad B
Cut 3 and 3 reversed

Grainline

Lily Pad C
Cut 4

Grainline

BACKGROUND GRID FOR *MONET WATER LILY*

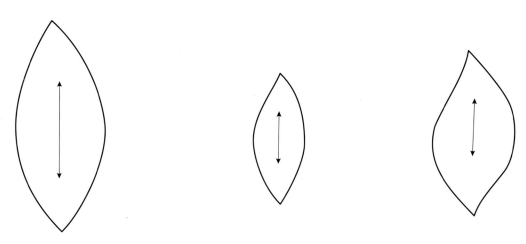

CUT VARIOUS SIZES OF WATER LILY PETALS FROM SOLID-COLORED COTTON FABRICS AND SHEER SPECIALTY FABRICS. SEAM ALLOWANCES NOT INCLUDED.

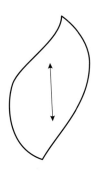

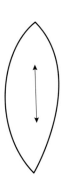

Colorwash Diamonds

by Jan Krentz
50" x 66"

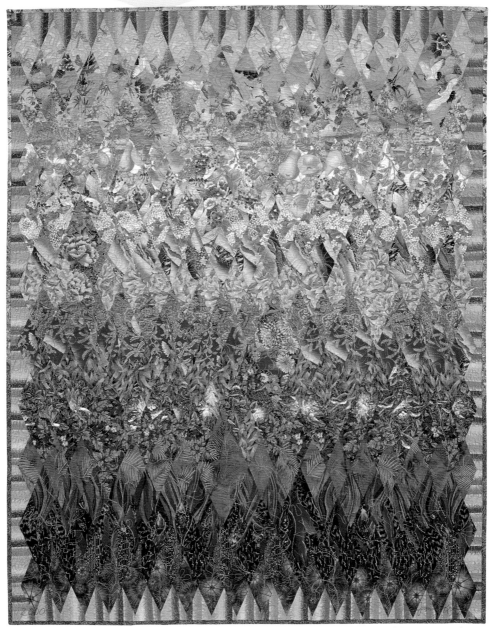

Machine quilted by Lisa Taylor.

This quilt is a fabric study using 45° diamonds. You will be using a large number of fabrics, in small quantities, to create your own composition. Adding to or subtracting from the number of diamonds in a row or the number of rows easily adjusts the quilt size. The diamond rows are shaded from light to dark. For variation, arrange fabrics in different combinations, such as light–medium–dark–medium– light or dark–medium–light–medium–dark.

111

FABRIC REQUIREMENTS

Equipment list (See page 33.)

⅜–½ yard of: 19 different patterned fabrics to total 7–9½ yards (see page 109 for fabric selection suggestions)

Border fabric: 1 yard of striped fabric

Backing: 3 yards

Binding: ½ yard—The binding for the quilt shown was made from leftover fabric that was pieced together to simulate the quilt's colorwash pattern.

Batting: 54" x 70"

Template plastic

CONSTRUCTION

1. Arrange the fabrics into a pleasing sequence. Create a numbered color chart by cutting a fabric swatch from each fabric and arranging them in the order you want in the quilt. You can refer to this chart as you place the diamonds on the grid.

2. Cut several 3" diamonds from each fabric (pages 43–45). The quilt shown uses 17–18 diamonds from each fabric.

3. Cut a 5½" diamond from each of several fabrics. The quilt shown uses 11 of these larger diamonds.

4. For the border, trace border patterns A, B, C, and D (page 112) onto template plastic. For the quilt shown, cut 18 A side border pieces, 34 B top and bottom border pieces, 2 C and 2 C reversed border corner pieces, and 2 D and 2 D reversed border corner pieces. Mark the dots onto the fabric pieces.

5. Place the diamonds on the design wall by following the color chart. Make the design as wide and long as you like; the featured quilt has 19 rows (top to bottom) and 18 diamonds (side to side), plus borders. Add the B border pieces to the top and bottom edges and add the A border pieces to the side edges.

6. Sew the diamonds into diagonal rows, including the border pieces at the ends of each row. When sewing on the border pieces, sew to the marked dot and backstitch. When the row contains a large diamond, sew the smaller diamonds into short row segments, sew the row segments together into pairs, and add a large diamond.

7. Sew 4–5 diamond rows together. To join rows, sew only between the marked dots on the border pieces and backstitch at each end. Sew border corner pieces D and C together before adding to the row.

8. To complete attaching the border pieces, sew from the quilt's edge to the dot and backstitch at each seam intersection. Carefully press the seams and return the sections to the design wall.

9. Sew larger sections together, pressing as you work. The final seam will join 2 halves to finish the whole quilt top.

10. Press the quilt top without distortion, moving the iron in the direction of the fabric's woven grain.

11. Add appliqué or embellishments if desired.

12. Baste the top, batting, and backing together. Quilt with an allover pattern by hand or machine. Add binding to finish the quilt.

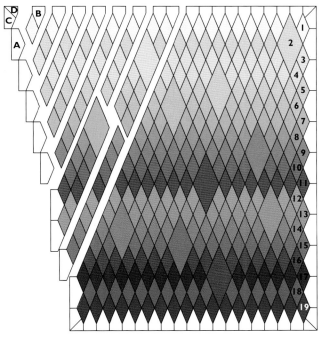

JOIN THE SECTIONS OF THE QUILT.

Morning Star's Garden
by **Christina Cormier**
55" x 66"

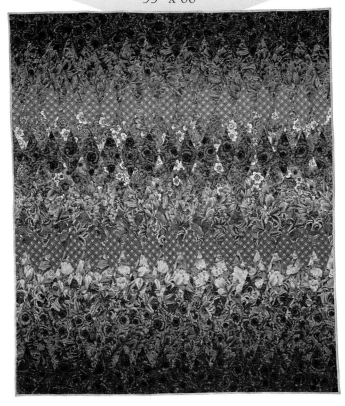

This quilt was inspired by Christina's own memories and love of nature and flowers. Morning Star is her Native American name, which was given to her by her husband's grandmother, who is also named Morning Star. The quilt reminds Christina of her own garden.

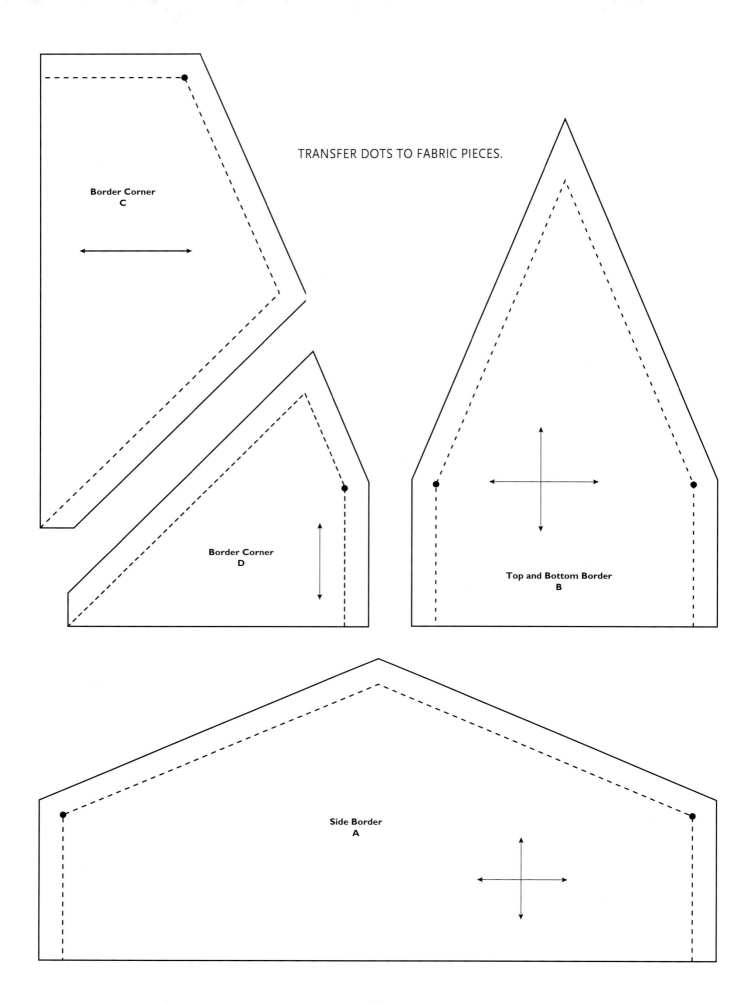

TRANSFER DOTS TO FABRIC PIECES.

Border Corner
C

Border Corner
D

Top and Bottom Border
B

Side Border
A

Fruitful Harvest Placemats

by Jan Krentz
20" x 16"

Design placemats to set the mood in your home. Fabric selection is the key to creating table accessories with a custom appeal. Coordinate cloth napkins to match the placemats for a special gift. Sewing small-scale gifts is a good way to use leftover batting.

Machine quilted and finished by Pam Kay

FABRIC SELECTION

LARGE-SCALE
PRINTED FABRICS
ARE IDEAL FOR
BRODERIE PERSE
APPLIQUÉ
DESIGNS.

FABRIC REQUIREMENTS FOR FOUR PLACEMATS

Supply list (See page 33.)

¼ yard each of 10–12 ivory tone-on-tone prints to total 2 ½ yards (*Note: Fat quarters work well because you can cut longer strips for the strip sets.*)

½–1 yard fabric with large-scale motif for appliqué designs

Backing: 1 ⅜ yards, cut into 4 pieces 22" x 18"

Binding: ⅝ yard

Lightweight, paper-backed fusible web: 1–1 ½ yards

Batting: 4 pieces 22" x 18"

CONSTRUCTION

1. Mark the bottom of a long acrylic ruler with 22.5° and 67.5° guidelines (page 40).

2. Lightly spray starch and press each fabric for stability during cutting and sewing.

3. Stack several single layers of the background fabrics face up on the cutting mat, orienting stripes and one-way designs in the same direction. Cut through all layers at a 22.5° or 67.5° angle (depending on the direction the diamonds will be oriented) to position the straight grain correctly in the diamonds (page 43). Cut 7–12 strips 2 ½" wide. Check the ruler alignment regularly.

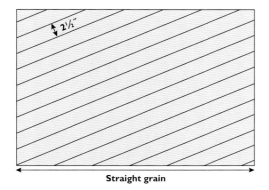

Straight grain

CUT THROUGH STACKED FABRICS AT 22.5°.
CHECK RULER ALIGNMENT REGULARLY.

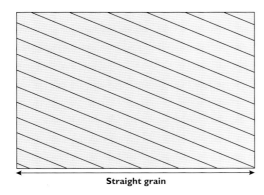

Straight grain

OPTION: YOU CAN ALSO CUT THROUGH STACKED FABRICS AT 67.5°.

4. Stack all fabrics right side up. Cut the ends of each strip at a 45° angle. Arrange the angled strips into rows, mixing the order of the fabrics.

5. Beginning at the ends with the 45° angle, cut, pin, and sew each strip to the next, creating strip sets of 6–8 strips each. Press the seams open. Do not stretch or distort the strip sets.

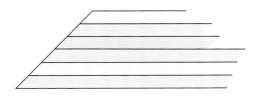

SEW STRIPS INTO STRIP SETS AND PRESS SEAMS OPEN.

6. From the strip sets, cut approximately 30 strips 2½" wide at a 45° angle. Align the 45° guide of your ruler with the bottom edge of the strip set or along a seamline. Adjust the ruler so the ruler's edge intersects with a seam, and cut a strip. Verify that the ruler is oriented properly and that the fabric grain runs through the center of the diamonds. (If the cut is not angled correctly, move to the adjacent corner and cut at a 45° angle in the opposite direction from the first cut.) Continually check the 45° angle. Cut single diamonds out of the short individual strips.

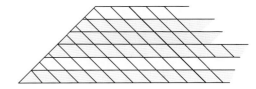

CUT 2 ½" STRIPS FROM PIECED STRIP SET, MAINTAINING A TRUE 45°.

7. Arrange the diamond rows, creating a rectangular shape. The short rows will fill in opposite corners of the rectangle. Longer diamond rows may be shortened by removing extra diamonds; short rows may be lengthened by adding spare diamonds.

8. Sew the diamond rows together, working diagonally from one corner to the opposite corner. Press the seams open. Align the 22.5° marks on the ruler with the seams; trim excess fabric from the edges, cutting the diamond composition into a 17" x 21" rectangle.

Create 4 rectangles.

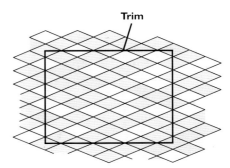

Trim

SEW DIAMOND ROWS INTO A COMPOSITION OF DIAMONDS;
FILL IN ROWS AS NEEDED. PRESS SEAMS OPEN;
TRIM INTO A RECTANGULAR SHAPE.

9. Fuse the adhesive web to the wrong side of the decorative motif fabric. Cut out the images, leaving a slight margin ($\frac{1}{16}"$–$\frac{1}{8}"$) surrounding each motif. (Leaving a slight margin allows you to use appliqué thread that matches the background color rather than needing several colors of thread to match each part of the motif.)

10. Remove the paper from each motif. Position the shapes artistically on the pieced placemat backgrounds. To preview the design placement, place a plate, flatware, a napkin, and a glass on the placemat. Is the image in a good location?

11. Once all motifs are positioned, fuse them to the diamond background following the manufacturer's directions.

12. Machine appliqué the motifs, stitching around each image to secure it to the background. If you are using a satin stitch, stabilize the fabric with one or more layers of stabilizer.

13. Remove excess stabilizer (if applicable). Press the placemats.

14. Layer the placemats with batting and backing. Securely pin all 3 layers together and machine quilt through all layers. Trim all placemats to 20" x 16". Add binding.

TIP:
Purchase extra fabric for cloth napkins to match either the appliqué cutouts or the binding. Allow 18" x 18" for each napkin. Finish the napkins with a rolled hem or machine overlock stitching.

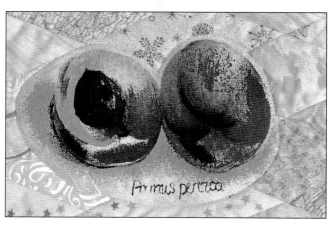

DETAILS OF *FRUITFUL HARVEST PLACEMATS*

Colorwash Lone Star

by Jan Krentz

34" x 34"

This star design features four rows of four diamonds per row.

Colorwash Lone Star is the link between *Lone Star Quilts & Beyond* and *Diamond Quilts & Beyond*. It is a joy to work with luscious fabrics, creating a gorgeous field of color! The 4 x 4 star requires small quantities of 19 fabrics; the optional 3 x 3 star (pages 123–124) is simpler and requires small quantities of 14 fabrics. Both stars feature Lone Star construction techniques. The quilt size includes the center star with setting squares and triangles. If you wish to add borders, plan yardage accordingly.

FABRIC SELECTION

Select fabrics with visual "texture" that share colors. If fabric #1 has blue with black, fabric #2 will contain blue or black plus a new color. Fabric #3 shares something in common with fabric #2, and so on. New colors are systematically introduced when each fabric relates to its neighbors. The fabrics blend well because they share colors and have patterned texture.

4 X 4 *COLORWASH LONE STAR*
(4 ROWS WITH 4 DIAMONDS PER ROW IN EACH DIAMOND UNIT)

FABRIC REQUIREMENTS

Supply list (See page 33.)

¼–½ yard each of 19 different fabrics—Refer to the diagram on page 122 for the location of each fabric within the quilt. Specific yardage requirements for each of the fabrics (using 2 ¼" cut diamonds) are as follows:

Fabrics 1, 5–15, 19: ¼ yard

Fabrics 2, 4, 16, 18: ⅜ yard

Fabrics 3, 17: ½ yard

Backing: 1 yard

Batting: 38" x 38"

Binding: ⅜ yard

PREPARATION

Place the fabrics in order from light to dark. Once you have established the "flow," or color gradation, of your fabrics, create a color chart by numbering 1–19. Paste a swatch of each fabric in order on the chart. Refer to this chart when cutting the strips and sewing them together into strip sets.

You must cut the strips *accurately*. Measure consistently from the fabric center fold, aligning the ruler's straight guidelines with the fold to ensure a perfectly perpendicular cut across the full width of the fabric (selvage to selvage). A strip length is approximately 42"–44" long (cut from selvage to selvage). *Subdivide* the full strips into fourths (2 ¼" wide x 10"–11" long). (Diamonds will not be cut individually.)

NOTE: If you prefer to make a larger Lone Star, choose a wider strip size and adjust the fabric quantities accordingly. When subdividing the strips, cut into thirds (13"–14" long), not fourths as is done for 2 ¼" strips.

Strip Size	Approximate Star Size
2 ½"	39"
3"	48 ½"

Background fabric placement in Jan's quilt is slightly different than the pattern specifications. Feel free to position fabrics according to your preferences or fabric quantity available.

CUTTING AND CONSTRUCTION

1. Cut the correct number of strips for the diamonds and subdivide according to the chart.

Fabric Number	Number of 2¼" Strips (selvage to selvage)	Number of Partial Strips	Yield Number of Diamonds (Diamonds will be cut after strips are sewn into strip sets.)
1 & 19	1	1	2
2 & 18	1	2	4
3 & 17, 9 & 11 4, 5, 6, 8, 12,	1	3	6
13, 14, 15, 16	1	4	8
Fabrics 7 & 10	2	5	10

2. Sort the strips into the following strip sets.

3. Stack all the fabric strips right side up. Cut the ends of each strip at a 45° angle.

STACK STRIPS. CUT ENDS OF EACH STRIP AT A 45° ANGLE.

4. Sew the strip sets together in order, allowing the ¼" tip to extend at the angled cut.

SEW STRIP SETS TOGETHER.

5. Press the seams open, using a light mist of spray starch to add body to the fabric.

6. Stack 2–4 strip sets, offsetting the upper edges by ½" to reduce the bulk of stacked seam allowances. Lay the ruler on the stacked strip sets and align the 45° guideline at the angled edge. Make a cleanup cut, removing the irregular edge.

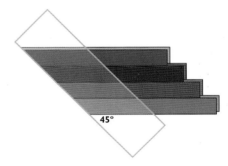

STACK STRIP SETS WITH ANGLED EDGES ALIGNED, OFFSETTING TOP EDGES BY ½". MAKE A CLEANUP CUT.

STRIP SETS FOR 4 X 4 STAR

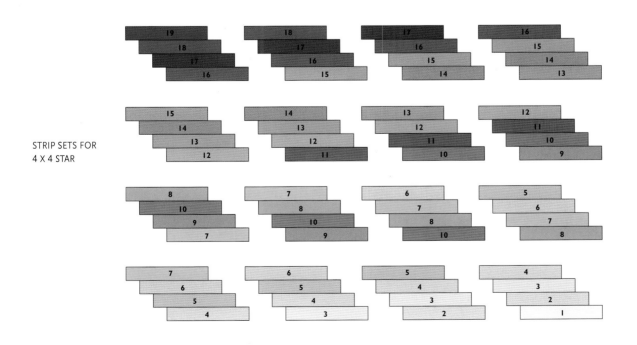

7. Begin cutting diagonal cuts through all thicknesses, the same width as the cut width of the strips you are using (2¼" strips require the angled cuts to be 2¼" wide). Make 2 angled cuts to create 2 rows of diamonds.

CUT STRIP SETS AT 45° ANGLE. REMOVE EXCESS WITH A CLEANUP CUT.
CUT 2 ROWS OF DIAMONDS FROM ALL STRIP SETS.

8. Arrange the rows of diamonds for your quilt design following your chart and the diagram on page 122. Using the tips on pages 51–53, pin the rows of diamonds together, matching intersections. Sew seams to create diamond units.

9. Measure between opposing parallel edges (Y) to determine the overall dimension of the diamond unit. (Note that this measurement does *not* equal the length of the outside edges.) Draw a blocking cloth with these measurements, maintaining a true 45° angle on both ends. Working on an ironing board or pressing board, align and pin the edges of the pieced diamond unit with the blocking cloth. Mist lightly with water and press the seams open. All 8 diamond units will be identical in size after blocking.

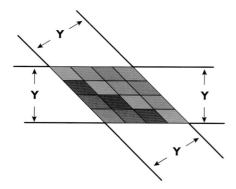

MEASURE OVERALL DIMENSIONS.

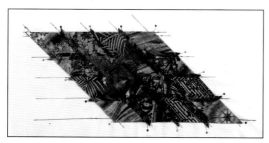

BLOCK DIAMOND UNITS.

TECHNIQUE TOOLBOX

Blocking is a very handy technique. Use it to shape diamond units, returning them to a symmetric 45° angle. Once all diamond units are the same shape and size, the quilt is easier to assemble without distortion.

10. Using a ruler and pencil or chalk marker, mark the tips and edges of each diamond with a ¼" intersection. Measure the length of the seamline between the marks. This measurement will be known as the X measurement.

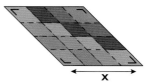

MARK TIPS AND EDGES OF DIAMONDS WITH ¼" INTERSECTIONS.
MEASURE BETWEEN MARKS TO DETERMINE X MEASUREMENT.

SETTING SQUARES AND TRIANGLES

1. Draw a square with X as the length of each side.

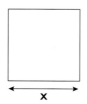

DRAW A SQUARE WITH X AS SIDE MEASUREMENT.

2. Add 1" to only 2 adjacent sides of the square. This will create extra fabric at the outer edge of the quilt for trimming and binding.

ADD 1" TO 2 EDGES OF SQUARE.

3. Draw 3 diagonal parallel lines across the block. The first line cuts the square in half, and the other 2 lines divide each of the triangle segments in half. This block is the master pattern for the corners.

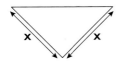

DRAW 3 DIAGONAL PARALLEL LINES ACROSS BLOCK.

4. Trace the block and cut into sections. Add a seam allowance to all sides of each section, except the edges with the 1" lines (the outside edge of the quilt.) Cut from the fabrics according to the diagram on page 122 and mark the dot. Piece the setting squares and press.

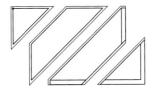

TRACE MASTER PATTERN. CUT SECTIONS APART.
ADD SEAM ALLOWANCE TO REMAINING 3 EDGES.

5. Draw 2 right triangles with X as the 2 shortest sides.

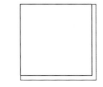

DRAW 2 TRIANGLES WITH X AS SIDE MEASUREMENT.

6. Add 1" to the longest side of both triangles, which will be the outside edge of the quilt.

ADD 1" TO LONGEST EDGE.

7. Draw 1 line parallel to the longest side, dividing the shortest sides in half.

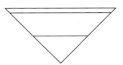

DRAW 1 PARALLEL LINE THROUGH EACH TRIANGLE.

8. On 1 triangle only, draw an additional line perpendicular to the longest side, dividing the triangle in half vertically.

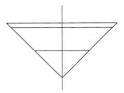

DIVIDE 1 TRIANGLE BY DRAWING A PERPENDICULAR LINE
FROM LONGEST SIDE TO 90° CORNER.

9. Trace and cut the sections apart. Add seam allowances on all sides except the edges with the 1" lines.

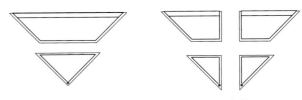

TRACE MASTER PATTERNS. CUT SECTIONS APART.
ADD SEAM ALLOWANCE TO REMAINING EDGES.

10. Layer fabrics right sides together and cut 2 pieces for each template shape. To achieve the best contrast between the star and the background, place light and dark fabrics according to the diagram on page 122. Mark the dots where indicated.

11. Assemble the star in the following manner, using the Y-seam technique. Pin seams, matching marked dots (∗) during assembly.

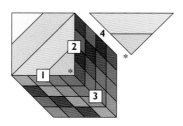

SEW SEAMS IN ORDER INDICATED TO CREATE 4 UNITS, STITCHING TO ¼" FROM CORNER, BACKSTITCHING AT ALL DOTS (∗).

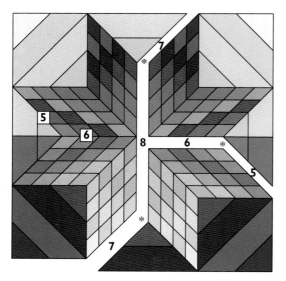

SEW QUARTER UNITS TOGETHER IN ORDER (SEAMS 5 AND 6), STITCHING TO ¼" FROM CORNER, BACKSTITCHING AT ALL DOTS (∗). SEW STAR HALVES TOGETHER (SEAM 7), STITCHING TO ¼" FROM THE CORNER, BACKSTITCHING AT DOT (∗). BASTE CENTER INTERSECTION WITH ¼" SEAMS. WHEN SATISFIED WITH ALIGNMENT, SEW CENTER SEAM (8), BACKSTITCHING AT DOT (∗).

12. Press the seams between each diamond unit to one side. Seam allowances will create a pinwheel in the center of the star, evenly distributing the bulk in the center. Press the seams toward the outer edges of the quilt top.

13. Baste the top, batting, and backing.

14. Quilt by hand or machine. If necessary, trim the quilt to clean up and straighten the edges. Bind the raw edges to finish the quilt.

PIECING DIAGRAM FOR 4 X 4 STAR

OPTIONAL 3 X 3 LONE STAR SETTING

COLORWASH LONE STAR BY KATHRYN VELTKAMP, 29" X 29".
PHOTO BY MELINDA C. HOLDEN. THIS QUILT WAS MADE
USING 2 1/2" DIAMONDS THAT ARE DIFFERENT FROM THE DIAMONDS
OF THE 4 X 4 PROJECT. DIRECTIONS ARE FOR 2 1/4" DIAMONDS.

Follow the instructions for the 4 x 4 *Colorwash Lone Star*, substituting the information below to make a 3 x 3 *Colorwash Lone Star*. A 3 x 3 star using 2 1/4" diamonds will make a 25 1/2" x 25 1/2" quilt.

3 X 3 COLORWASH LONE STAR
(3 ROWS WITH 3 DIAMONDS IN EACH DIAMOND UNIT)

FABRIC REQUIREMENTS AND CUTTING

1/4–1/2 yard each of 14 different fabrics—Refer to the diagram on page 124 for the location of each fabric within the quilt. Specific yardage requirements for each of the fabrics (using 2 1/4" cut diamonds) are as follows:

Fabrics 5–10: 1/8 yard

Fabrics 1–3, 12–14: 1/4 yard

Fabrics 4, 11: 3/8 yard

Backing: 1 yard

Batting: 33" x 33"

Binding: 3/8 yard

PREPARATION

Place the fabrics in order from light to dark. Once you have established the "flow," or color gradation, of your fabrics, create a color chart by numbering from 1–14. Paste a swatch of each fabric in order on the chart.

NOTE: If you prefer to make a larger Lone Star, choose a wider strip size and adjust the fabric quantities accordingly. When subdividing the strips, cut into thirds (not fourths, as is done for 2 1/4" strips).

Strip Size	Approximate Star Size
2 1/2"	29"
3"	36"

You must cut the strips *accurately*. Measure consistently from the fabric center fold, aligning the ruler's straight guidelines with the fold to ensure a straight cut across the full width of the fabric (selvage to selvage). A strip length is approximately 42"–44" long (cut from selvage to selvage). *Subdivide* the full strips into fourths (2 1/4" wide x 10"–11" long). (Diamonds will not be cut individually.)

CUTTING AND CONSTRUCTION

1. Cut the correct number of strips for the diamonds and subdivide according to the chart.

Fabric Number	Number of 2¼" Strips (selvage to selvage)	Number of Partial Strips	Yield Number of Diamonds (Diamonds will be cut after strips are sewn into strip sets.)
1 & 14	1	1	2
2 & 13	1	2	4
3 & 12, 4 &11, 5–10	1	4	8

2. Follow the steps for making the 4 x 4 star. You may choose to draft the same setting squares and triangles as for the 4 x 4 star, as Kathryn Veltkamp did.

PIECING DIAGRAM FOR 3 X 3 STAR

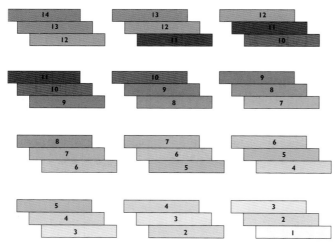

STRIP SETS FOR 3 X 3 STAR

Index

About the Author

Jan Krentz is a nationally known author, quilt instructor, and designer. Her lifelong passion for sewing and needlework led her to quiltmaking during her high school years. Jan began teaching quiltmaking in the mid-1970s and was an active member of her local quilt guild. She was selected as the 1998 Teacher of the Year by *Professional Quilter* magazine. She teaches nationwide for quilting guilds, retreats, and seminars and appears on television and in magazines.

Jan is a prolific quilter who inspires students of all skill levels to achieve solid quiltmaking techniques while boldly expanding into new uses of color and design. Her specialty is working with star quilts and 45° diamond designs of all kinds. She prefers the structure of pieced designs that are further embellished and quilted. Her first two books, published by C&T Publishing, are *Lone Star Quilts & Beyond* and *Hunter Star Quilts & Beyond*.

Jan lives with her husband, Don, and their family in Poway, a community near San Diego, California.

Please refer to her website for her teaching schedule, quiltmaking tips, and product information.

Jan Krentz
P.O. Box 686
Poway, CA 92074-0686
www.jankrentz.com
jan@jankrentz.com

OTHER BOOKS BY JAN KRENTZ

for more information

For a Fussy Cutter diamond guide or a free catalog:
C&T Publishing, Inc.
P.O. Box 1456
Lafayette, CA 94549
800-284-1114
email: ctinfo@ctpub.com
website: www.ctpub.com

for fabric and supplies

Cotton Patch Mail Order
3404 Hall Lane
Dept. CTB
Lafayette, CA 94549
800-835-4418
925-283-7883
email: quiltusa@yahoo.com
website: www.quiltusa.com